alwa

**Please check
in back for CD**

The law changes, but Nolo is on top of it! We of
ways to make sure you and your Nolo products a.

1 **Nolo's Legal Updater**
We'll send you an email whenever a new edit
published! Sign up at **www.nolo.com/legalup**

2 **Updates @ Nolo.com**
Check **www.nolo.com/update** to find recent changes
in the law that affect the current edit

3 **Nolo Customer Service**
To make sure that this edition of the book is the most
recent one, call us at **800-728-3555** and ask one of
our friendly customer service representatives.
Or find out at **www.nolo.com**.

DATE DU

NOLO

please note

We believe accurate, plain-English legal information should help
you solve many of your own legal problems. But this text is not a
substitute for personalized advice from a knowledgeable lawyer.
If you want the help of a trained professional—and we'll always
point out situations in which we think that's a good idea—consult
an attorney licensed to practice in your state.

1st edition

A Judge's Guide to Divorce

Uncommon Advice From the Bench

by Judge Roderic Duncan

FIRST EDITION	FEBRUARY 2007
Editor	BARBARA KATE REPA
Book Design	SUSAN PUTNEY
Cover Design	SUSAN PUTNEY
Production	JESSICA STERLING
Proofreading	ROBERT WELLS
Index	BAYSIDE INDEXING SERVICE
Printing	CONSOLIDATED PRINTERS, INC.

Duncan, Roderic, 1932-
    A judge's guide to divorce : uncommon advice from the bench / by Roderic Duncan.
        p. cm.
    ISBN-13: 978-1-4133-0568-5 (alk. paper)
    ISBN-10: 1-4133-0568-7 (alk. paper)
      1. Divorce--Law and legislation--United States--Popular works. 2. Divorce
suits--United States--Popular works. I. Title.

KF535.Z9D857 2007
346.7301'66--dc22

                                                    2006047211

Dedication

To Carol Thompson, my wife and exhilarating companion, who has a sparkle in her eye as she handles her many other roles as a proud mother, loving grandma and talented gardener, decorator, cook, and Airedale enthusiast. Her expertise as a mental health professional and child custody evaluator has been a major force in shaping this book.

Acknowledgments

This book was the bright idea of Nolo Acquisitions Editor Marcia Stewart, who guided me through preparing the first proposed table of contents. I consulted my former law school professor Herma Hill Kay, who thought I was up to the task, and off I went. Professor Kay, a distinguished family law author and former dean of Boalt Hall School of Law, has provided some coaching along the way.

It became clear that Nolo was strongly behind the project when Managing Editor Janet Portman assigned Barbara Kate Repa to edit this book. She is an excellent lawyer, a whiz at Internet research, a very successful author on her own, and an editor extraordinaire. Working with me presented her with some unusual challenges. As a former newspaper reporter, I had stored away a ton of stories about "interesting cases" that had come through my court over 20 years. It took a strong and talented editor to sift out a few that belonged in the book. All I can say is her choices were always right—and we are still friends. I am deeply grateful.

Madelyn Herman, chief of Knowledge and Information Services at the National Center for State Courts, provided me with invaluable help in learning what is happening across the country in family law courts.

For their role in some of the stories that made it past Ms. Repa's editing, I want to thank Justice Marc Poche, Justice Donald B. King, and attorney Jane Bond Moore (who is the lawyer in the story about the woman who for a while didn't want any part of her husband's pension). And I'd like to recognize some great family law judges who share with me the joy of doing divorce court: Judge James Garbolino, Judge Thomas Murphy, and Judge Robert A. Schnider.

Finally, I want to thank again my diligent courtroom staff for ten years: Nancy Regas, Bob Artis, Carol Gilbert, and Leo Tungohan.

Foreword

Divorce is one of the most painful experiences a person can have. I know that from my own experiences getting divorced—and also from serving as a divorce judge for many years. During my time on the bench, I signed judgments and orders in at least 25,000 divorce cases. And since retiring, I have taught, written, and privately judged in the field. I have consulted and worked with some of the top legal and psychological experts on divorce in the country.

I know a lot about divorce.

This wrenching process of splitting up a marriage is no longer the unusual event that took place in a few families only occasionally a few decades ago. Now, close to half of the marriages in the United States end up in divorce court. That amounts to more than a million divorces a year.

Divorce in America is actually made up of two separate painful experiences. The first takes place when one or both spouses decide to end the beautiful dream that caused them to decide to get married. The second usually begins when they enter the court system and appear before a judge who will make orders about many aspects of their lives before eventually restoring them to the status of being single. The court process may take only a few minutes or, as in one case over which I presided, 12 years—and still counting.

The disturbing thing that I learned as a divorce court judge is that most people getting divorced know very little about the legal side of the process that often controls their finances, the custody of their children, and the ownership of their homes, their automobiles, and their investments. And very many of these people—some represented by lawyers, some not—stumble through the divorce maze, making mistakes that cause the process to be more expensive, time-consuming, and painful than it need be. Not surprisingly, most come away unhappy with their experience.

You may be curious about why anyone would choose to work for so long in what is often such an unhappy setting. Most of my colleagues on the bench were clear in wanting to avoid being assigned to preside over divorce court. Both the issues and the litigants are frequently difficult.

But for me, the appeal of working in divorce court was similar to the tug that many emergency room doctors, police officers, firefighters, and ambulance personnel feel: There is something rewarding about dealing with people in trouble and in helping them find their ways back to a better lives.

I looked forward to every day I served as a divorce court judge. And as I drove home in the evening, I could almost always think of at least a person or two whose circumstances were at least a little better as a result of their appearance in my court.

This book synthesizes the best of those experiences—and warns against the worst. If you and your spouse read it with open minds before you become too tangled in the rather imperfect court system, you can be one of the divorcing participants who come away without the stress and the deep scars that are carried by so many others.

State laws provide for many cumbersome procedures that often mean divorcing couples must wait for months before they make even their first court appearance. But there are ways to avoid this thicket of delays and conflict.

This book advises you to do everything you can to keep your divorce out of court. While this route requires that both spouses agree to follow it, for many divorcing couples, it is realistic and possible.

Still, there are cases where anger or injury may make it impossible for you to use the processes described here for avoiding the court system. So the book also includes important advice based on many years of working in and around the court system about how to navigate through the courts with or without the help of a divorce lawyer.

In short, this book can help you have the best possible divorce.

That's why I wrote it.

Table of Contents

How to Use This Book

10 Enforce Orders and Deal With Violence Legally

11 Get On With Your Life

Index

How to Use This Book

This book assumes that you or your spouse have decided—or are seriously considering—getting a divorce. Unless your marriage is what is known as a covenant marriage available in a few states—including Arizona, Arkansas, and Louisiana—either of you can obtain a divorce without showing that the other person was at fault.

This book explains how to obtain the best possible divorce in your particular situation.

The first and most important decision you can make in getting the best possible divorce is to keep your case out of court. To understand why, read **Chapter 1, Stay Out of Divorce Court If You Can.** The proceedings in divorce court are governed by the same rules that control every other type of case that goes to court in the United States. These rules often turn what should be a quick and inexpensive end to a marriage into a long, costly battle that is entirely unnecessary.

Some simple steps that will allow you to keep your divorce out of court are set out in **Chapter 2, Consider Alternatives to Divorce Court.** Many wise couples sit down around their kitchen tables and reach agreements on how to resolve the issues in their divorces. If that won't work for you, this chapter also explains mediation and collaborative law, both of which are immensely more satisfying alternatives than divorcing in court.

But unfortunately, there are cases in which the good advice in the first chapters will fall on deaf ears. Your spouse—or maybe even you—for any or all the reasons explained in Chapter 2, may want a war instead of a settlement. In that case, **Chapter 3, If You Must Go to Court, Follow These Tips,** will help you avoid the mistakes many people make in presenting their cases in court. Some of these mistakes cause them to lose their homes or custody of their children. Others are simply expensive.

Chapter 4, Don't Get Hung Up on Fairness, is for everyone. It deals with a little known fact about divorce courts: They sometimes deliver unjust results. Divorce courts are required to apply the laws of the state legislature and of higher appellate courts—even when the people involved and the judge presiding over the case may all believe the result is not fair.

Chapter 5, Know How and Where to Get Legal Help, deals with the question of whether to get legal help of various kinds—and how to find it. It is relevant to those who plan to negotiate their cases out of court—and especially for those who are forced into court because of a complicated situation or an uncompromising spouse. For the adventuresome, it explains how to do some basic legal research on your own. If you want to hire a lawyer and can't afford one, the chapter gives you some leads on how to get inexpensive or free legal assistance. And it explains how to choose the best lawyer for you and how to manage your relationship with him or her.

The next several chapters deal with specific subjects at the heart of many divorces:

- dividing your possessions (**Chapter 6, When Dividing Your Property, Don't Hide the Ball**)
- support (**Chapter 7, Don't Waste Time Fighting Alimony**)
- child support (**Chapter 8, Know What to Expect in Child Support**), and
- child custody (**Chapter 9, Settle Child Custody and Visitation Issues Sanely**).

Sadly, **Chapter 10, Enforce Orders and Deal With Violence Legally,** may turn out to be more important to you than you can now imagine. It deals with a not uncommon situation in which your spouse or ex-spouse violates a provision of a court order or judgment. This may be the failure to make a support payment or to have your child ready to be picked up at the time visitation is scheduled. It may apply if your spouse has been ordered to stop harassing you on the telephone or coming by your job or home, or if the angst of the situation escalates into violent behavior. It is important to use the court's powers to punish such violations—and this chapter explains how to do it.

Finally, **Chapter 11, Get On With Your Life,** is intended for all people who get divorced, whether in a friendly settlement or a long court battle. It contains advice on how to combat the stress you are sure to experience and how to maintain some perspective about this divorce being just one small chapter in the larger book of your life. It also points you to resources that are available to help you recover from the strain of a divorce.

Stay Out of Divorce Court If You Can

Unless you're very lucky, you probably won't be able to totally avoid having to go into divorce court in the process of getting divorced, but you should do your best to make as little contact as possible with this jungle of bickering people, long delays, and harried and sometimes uninterested judges. This may sound like strange advice coming from a judge who happily spent most of his judicial career sitting behind the bench in a divorce court, but it is the best advice I can give you. I loved the work, but saw over and over again that the system stinks. Whatever you do, try to keep your divorce out of divorce court.

Later chapters of this book offer lots of advice about how you can keep your divorce out of divorce court. This one explains why.

A Look Inside the System

Divorce courts operate with the same basic rules used by the courts that deal with car accidents, disputes between giant corporations, and criminal charges from petty theft to murder. Unfortunately, these rules do not work well in solving the disputes that arise in the process of ending a marriage.

In most states, divorce courts are a branch of the local trial court—called the Circuit, Superior, or District Court. In Delaware, Hawaii, Massachusetts, New York, Rhode Island, South Carolina, and Vermont, these courts are entirely separate from the rest of the court system and are called Family Courts or something similar. Regardless of how they are labeled, the operating and procedural rules in these courts are the backbone of what is called "the adversary system." It is built on the ancient British practice of having lawyers representing each side of a case fight as hard as they can to defeat their opponents at a trial. The theory is that after hearing the evidence and argument from these lawyers, a neutral judge or jury will figure out who is telling the truth and reach a just decision as to which side wins.

Matters such as divorces were handled in merry olde England by officials known as chancellors in courts that were connected to the church. Juries were not used in these Chancery Courts—and to this day, juries are almost never used in United States divorce courts. Texas is an exception. But even there, jury trials are used only occasionally in divorces. More often then not, a Texas lawyer will use the threat of demanding a jury trial as part of an elaborate game of Chicken, as in: "If you don't agree to lower your claim for alimony, I'm going to insist that this case be decided by a jury."

In all states, especially in cases that involve big bucks, each side will normally spend months getting prepared for the trial. The lawyers will investigate the facts, take depositions of important witnesses, and subpoena records from banks, employers, and any other source they believe has relevant evidence. They may prepare charts and elaborate electronic presentations to illustrate their arguments. They skirmish in pretrial hearings to exclude harmful evidence and to narrow the issues that can be considered in court. All of this is in preparation for a trial that—if it occurs at all—will usually take place at least a year or two after the case was filed.

This is the way disputes that land in American courts are resolved. You can see dramatizations of these courtroom battles on television. One channel even devotes much of its time presenting scenes from splashy trials all day, every day. The system actually works relatively well to resolve a legal situation that doesn't involve divorce—such as a murder case, a major car accident, or a claim of medical malpractice. And if the stakes are high and the winner is going to be determined in a trial lasting days or weeks before a jury, the need for all of that painstaking preparation is understandable.

A Glossary of Divorce Jargon

Each state has its own rules spelling out the procedures to obtain a divorce. Here is a brief description of the terms you're likely to encounter in connection with divorce—and the legalities generally involved in each one.

Default divorce. One of the spouses prepares the papers for a standard divorce and gets a summons issued by the court. The other spouse is served with these papers, which specify that he or she has a certain number of days—usually 30—to have a voice in the terms of the divorce by filing an answer. If no response is filed within the time allotted, the spouse who originally filed asks the court to declare a default. If the court clerk finds everything in order, the default is entered and the divorce is granted. In some states, the whole process can occur without a personal court appearance by either of the people being divorced. A judge will normally review the divorce provisions to make sure they appear to be fair. Some people who have reached a total agreement and really trust their spouses use this method to avoid paying a second filing fee and to get the divorce processed quickly.

Legal separation. This is an alternative to divorce that is usually used, by people who have religious restrictions on divorce or financial advantages to remaining legally married. Like a standard divorce, it has provisions for support, child custody, and division of the couple's property; however, the parties remain legally married. In New York, filing a legal separation agreement can be the first step in obtaining a divorce a year later, without a showing that either spouse is at fault for causing the divorce.

Simplified, summary, or expedited divorce. Some states have streamlined procedures that go by one of these titles. They require special forms and are frequently limited to cases in which couples have been married for less than five years, have no children, own no real estate, and where neither is asking for support from the other. There are often additional requirements, which vary from state to state.

Uncontested divorce. One of the spouses files the necessary papers for a standard divorce, the other files the required answer—and then the parties present the court with a written settlement agreement including the terms for support, child custody, and division of their property. The package is presented to the court, reviewed by a judge and the divorce is granted, often without either of the parties having to appear in court. Some states have a similar provision that allows the parties to file a joint petition for divorce.

Why Divorces Don't Belong in Court

Unfortunately, the traditional adversary system works very poorly when the issue before the court is the breakup of a family. In such cases, hours spent preparing for trial and parading witnesses on and off the stand could be spent much more productively if the people involved would calmly discuss and settle the issues somewhere other than a courtroom.

But once divorce lawyers have taken a case into court, they are required to rely upon the historical underpinnings of the adversary system, and normally have little choice but to follow the same procedures as business and criminal lawyers in getting ready for their trials.

They sometimes have the family's children studied by experts to determine how much time should be spent with each of the parents. They may also enlist accountants to examine the couple's assets and appraisers to evaluate the family business, home, and vehicles. They often take the depositions of these experts and question each of the spouses under oath in front of a court reporter about their income, what it costs to keep the household running for an average month, and many other personal subjects. They try to develop facts that show that one of the spouses is inept as a parent—or, if that fails, how flawed he or she is as a person. Sometimes they hire a private detective to follow one of the parties in the hope of garnering information about damning conduct.

Then, a year or so after filing a case, the lawyers on both sides will organize their anticipated trial presentations. They may have been discussing settlement for some time, but as their trial date approaches, the intensity of settlement negotiations increase.

In more than nine out of ten cases, a settlement is reached before the day of trial. And in an amazing number of cases, the settlement is reached only a few days or hours before the trial is scheduled to begin. Settlement often comes in an exchange of letters or telephone calls between the lawyers. Other times, it will come as a result of a meeting among the lawyers and their clients in a conference room. Many settlements occur in a judge's chambers—a fancy English name for an office, usually with a private bathroom, next to the courtroom—at a settlement conference scheduled by the court just before the trial date. But the bottom line is that almost all cases wind up settling, not actually going to trial.

Most divorcing couples could avoid all of this legal wrangling and get on with their lives much more quickly and inexpensively by settling their disputes somewhere other than in a courtroom.

And you probably won't be surprised to learn that the divorce courts are riddled with a number of additional drawbacks—from high costs to disgruntled judges—that underscore why they are unfitting places to end a marriage

High Costs

Lawyers, accountants, and child custody evaluators often will spend a ton of the divorcing couple's money preparing for a trial that is highly unlikely to occur.

Of course, a lawyer who relied upon a settlement that didn't occur and then was forced to go to trial unprepared would do his or her client a great disservice. So, months before trial, many lawyers will describe the legal situation for their clients in a speech that goes something like this: "This is not an easy case and if you want to increase our chances of winning, I am going to need to hire several expert witnesses to go over your finances and your spouse's finances, to evaluate the stock options your spouse has earned, and to establish that your spouse is not a very good parent. It will cost between $10,000 and $20,000 to hire these experts. But I think that if you want to win, you should do it. What do you say?" Many clients cave in and agree to pay the costs of escalating the fight.

In cases in which at least one of the parties earns a substantial amount of money and there is a major disagreement about when their children will be with each of the parents, it is not unusual for the lawyers' and psychologists' bills to reach $20,000 on that issue alone. If the parties can't pay fees of this type upfront, the case will be presented less expertly.

In a recent article in *The New Yorker* magazine, a prominent Manhattan divorce lawyer stated that his fee is $550 an hour with a minimum retainer of $25,000. Another lawyer is quoted in the story as saying that big cases are likely to be "a battle of forensic accountants." In one case, he said, the accountants had billed more than $1.5 million. Of course, these sorts of bills do not arise in garden variety divorces. But any contested divorce is expensive and can be as costly as one spouse wants to make it.

Antagonism and Angst

In addition to being outrageously expensive, the present legal system needlessly heightens the negative emotions of the divorcing spouses by purposefully pitting one side against the other.

Many more people than you would guess maintain at least some sort of a friendly relationship with a former spouse after a divorce. But that is highly unlikely if the two of you go through a contested trial.

Harm to Children

Chapters 8 and 9 include detailed discussions of the legalities and practicalities of child support, custody, and visitation. But for now, realize that in addition to what it does to each of the parties, a contested divorce trial ultimately ends up causing terrible damage to any children caught in the crossfire.

Here are a few truths I have learned over the years.

- Unless one parent has acted particularly ugly, many children live for at least a little while after the break-up with the secret hope their parents will get back together. It is not a thought they often share with anyone except, perhaps, their best friends. They look for little hints that an impending divorce will go away, and pale when they hear one parent badmouth the other.

- For children, the prospect of their parents splitting up is so primal that the first thing many worry about is whether there is going to be a roof over their heads and food on the table once one of their parents moves out of the family home.

- Being confronted with the life changes brought on because "Mommy and Daddy don't love each other anymore" is frequently a shock from which a child never quite recovers. There are counselors who can help a child get over such feelings, but that sort of help is not as available or used as often as it should be.

Court battles about how much support will be paid, who is to get which car, and how much time each parent will have with the children all have some unpleasantness about them. A wife may suggest that her husband has some money coming into his business under the table. A husband might argue that his wife's long distance telephone bills are excessive. They both may claim their children are uncomfortable around Mom or Dad's new friends.

Resolving these disputed issues out of court can frequently be accomplished quietly and respectfully around a kitchen table or in a conference room. But having a judge decide these sorts of issues after hearing each of the parents testify in the formal public courtroom often fosters anger, embarrassment, and hurt feelings that are bound to be carried home to children who live there.

Pretty soon, "Daddy" becomes "Your Father." "Mom" is "Your Mother." Messages are handled by notes sealed in envelopes which the children are asked to carry between two armed camps. Doors that used to be closed quietly are now slammed shut. And a child's plea for a new pair of sneakers just like a friend has may be answered with: "Ask your father; he has all the money."

But I have seen enough of the real success stories to feel a surge of deep respect for spouses who work to maintain a healthy relationship. In most divorces, both spouses usually have many reasons to be hurt and angry about their former partners. But a more reasoned approach is to send a child off for a visit with: "Have a great time with your Dad—and tell him I said hello." Or: "Your friend Ralph's new sneakers look great. I'll talk to your Mom and see if we can find a way to get some for you."

Dreaming of a Better System

From time to time, people lobby to take divorces out of the adversary system and deal with them in a way that recognizes their unique nature. Reform of this system may benefit your grandchildren—if, heaven forbid, they ever get divorced. But unfortunately, that isn't going to help you get divorced today.

As noted by Donald B. King, a retired judge and coauthor of a three-volume set for lawyers on divorce law, titled *Family Law* (The Rutter Group): "Our present system is not only impersonal, inhumane, production line justice, it fails to help people at one of the most critical points in their lives. Indeed, all too often, those who the law requires to go through the system are worse off at the end than they were when they entered it."

King's criticism includes the charge that the system "not only allows people to fight, it encourages it, even for those who . . . do not want to fight."

Americans for Divorce Reform (www.divorcereform.org), a consumer group that supports efforts to reduce divorce, urges that premarital counseling should be required for couples before a marriage license is issued. The group also supports making it more difficult to get divorced because it believes more people would work out their marital problems and stay together if the divorce procedure wasn't so easy.

A quick survey of how other nations handle divorce, if they even allow it, does not indicate any panaceas out there.

Long Delays

Another reason that divorce courts don't work well is that, in comparison to the rest of the court system, they are often seriously understaffed both by judges and support people, which can cause long delays in processing cases.

In most areas, presiding judges, who decide which judge is going to sit in what courtroom, need to keep the criminal courts processing the very visible cases of people charged with breaking the law, so a large portion of the court's resources are directed to the criminal division. And the lawyers involved in the accident cases and business disputes use their considerable influence in the state legislature and elsewhere to have as many courts as possible devoted to their trials. Family and juvenile courts have lower profiles than regular civil and criminal courts and are often overwhelmed by backlogs of cases waiting for hearing.

"Short cause cases" involving simple issues such as requests to grant temporary support before trial are usually scheduled to be heard in the mornings in most divorce courts. But because of the large number of such cases, many are frequently bumped until the afternoon, the time often reserved for contested "long cause" trials. And some cases set in afternoon get put over to the next day or the next week—and sometimes to the next month or longer.

You may have to wait a very long time for a hearing on the day you have been told to come to court—and at the end of the wait, you may be told to come back on another day.

WARNING

You'll pay while you wait. If you've hired a lawyer to help handle your divorce, he or she will charge you for the time spent waiting for your case to be called. I still have a little plaque that a legal publishing company sent me when I graduated from law school in 1961. It contains a drawing of Abraham Lincoln with a quotation: "A lawyer's time is his stock in trade." And a lawyer's waiting time frequently is charged the same as his or her trial time.

The length of time it takes to get a divorce case from filing to judgment is one of the major complaints all divorce judges hear about the system. And there are no signs of that situation improving substantially in the near future.

The obvious solution is to assign more judges and staff to handle family law cases. But there are no indications that presiding judges are going to pull trial judges from other functions and assign them to divorce court. Assignments of staff that might help shorten proceedings aren't likely to increase, either. Increased financial support from the state legislatures would take care of the problem, but the cause does not have political support. Many people in the court system consider divorce courts as the poor cousin of the system. They would rather not hear about all of the "unfortunate people" trying to get their divorce cases to trial—and concentrate instead on flashier causes.

Overloaded Calendars

The fact that divorce courts are understaffed not only accounts for long delays in hearings, but it often means that those appearing in court have a dizzyingly short time to present their cases, requiring judges to make swift decisions, without much time for consideration.

For example, on almost every morning of the ten years I sat in divorce court, three hours were allotted to hear the evidence and make orders regarding child custody and support in the 35 cases or so that were scheduled. Some of them would settle through negotiations lawyers reached in the hallway in front of the courtroom, but many did not. For those that didn't settle, the rules provided up to 20 minutes for hearing each case. But on mornings when there were a large number of cases scheduled, I could only devote ten minutes to many of them.

A Quick—and Haunting—Decision

In a case I handled several years ago, a couple with few assets between them appeared without lawyers to argue the husband's motion to have the children come live with him from Monday to Friday every week during the school year. The existing order, granted a year earlier, provided that the mother was to have primary custody and the father was to have visitation every other weekend. The parents had been referred to a court child custody counselor for a recommendation. But the counselor took a dive and reported that the matter was too complex to evaluate in the short time allotted.

The only options were to hear the evidence quickly or put the case over to a day at least a month away. Something told me the case shouldn't wait, so I had the parties sworn and asked the father why he was seeking greater time with the children. Quickly, he told me was a garbage man with no prospects for getting a higher-paying job because he lacked a college education. Appearing very sincere, he said he thought a good education would guarantee better jobs for his children. He said the mother wasn't getting the children to school on time and he showed me their report cards, which indicated a huge number of absences and tardies.

I asked the mother for an explanation and she went off on a bizarre story about being afraid the father's coworkers were spying on her from the garbage trucks that went by outside her house.

By then, I needed to get moving to deal with the other cases waiting to be heard. I had to make a decision. Fast.

Intuition told me the children's best interests were with the father, so I took a deep breath and ordered that he should have full weekday custody during the school year, with the mother having visitation every weekend. The whole matter had taken about 25 minutes—hardly enough time to gather enough evidence on an issue likely to make a huge impact on the young children's lives.

To this day, I don't know what happened next or whether my intuition was right, how the children fared, or whether they are safe and attending school. The legal system did not provide an adequate opportunity for me to do the right thing.

Wrong Decisions

Even when the parties have good lawyers and enough money to provide the court with tons of information and professional advice on who should have the custody of a child or how much support should be paid, there is the possibility that even a well-meaning, experienced family law judge will rule for the wrong side. And an inexperienced judge or one who is disgruntled with the assignment to divorce court may make a decision that is just plain factually or legally wrong.

Some examples help illustrate.

- In the course of divorcing, a small business owner may come to court without financial records and swear that the business is losing money. Her spouse might testify that she does a lot of business in cash "under the table." The judge must set child support and alimony based on a conclusion about just what the business really earns on an average month. And where the records are incomplete or falsified, a judge may end up believing the wrong party. As a result, the court order may provide inadequate or overly generous support.

- The judge who must decide which parents the children will live with will never know them as well as their parents do. And that judge will never know for sure what happened during a violent incident that occurred behind closed doors six weeks ago. Testimony given in court often varies widely between two witnesses. Sometimes there are discrepancies or other indications about truthfulness at a hearing, but at other times the ultimate decision is based on little more than a judge's gut feeling. I know that in some cases, my gut must have been wrong and that a child's life was probably affected adversely.

- When dividing a couple's possessions, the evidence may show that a large sum of money disappeared from the family bank account several years ago. The husband may testify that he and his wife jointly agreed to put the money into a restaurant that later failed. The wife may believe that the husband spent it on a suspicious "business trip" to Las Vegas that included several nights in a luxury hotel with a new girlfriend. Nobody has documents to verify their claims. The judge can't make an investigation, but must decide based upon the incomplete evidence at hand.

One of the many sad but common scenes in divorce court is the husband or wife who walks into court with a relaxed, almost cocky look, apparently convinced of winning a great victory. Often this is because a lawyer who doesn't really know the way around divorce court very well assured him or her that the case was a sure thing. Then the testimony begins. And on cross-examination, the opposing lawyer will start asking some difficult questions. The "sure thing" begins to crumble and the formerly cocky lawyer spends a lot of time conferring and whispering with the formerly cocky client.

Whatever the reason, when you let a judge decide an important matter in your life, understand there are few "sure things" in a court hearing— and there is always a possibility that you will not prevail. (See Chapter 4, Don't Get Hung Up on Fairness, for more on this.)

> **WARNING**
>
> **There are no special truth-seeking tools.** Occasionally, various experts present classes to judges, purporting to teach them how they can tell whether a person is lying by evaluating facial clues. For example, one such class presented videos of people—one of whom was Oliver North, of Iran-Contra infamy—testifying about things that later clearly turned out not to be true. The instructor pointed out how a facial tic appeared every time North was telling a lie. The connection was clear, but not particularly helpful in evaluating the truthfulness of a person sitting in the witness box in a courtroom. To make it work, a person would have to put a witness through hours of testing of facial movements that occurred during lies.

One Judge's Lethal Decision

The most horrible decision I know about occurred when I was working as a lawyer in an Oakland law firm years ago, when a client was involved in a child custody dispute in nearby San Francisco.

I argued his case before a respected judge who was later appointed to the federal court. I produced some evidence indicating the client was a straight arrow and a good father—and that the mother appeared to be somewhat unstable. The mother took the witness stand, trashed the father, and then testified convincingly about her stellar mothering ability. The judge believed her and granted the mother the primary custody of the parties' children.

Ten days later, the local newspaper reported that the mother had driven her car off a cliff, killing herself and the children. My first reaction was to tear the story from the newspaper and send it to the judge with a note about his decision. The senior partner in my law firm convinced me to change my mind, pointing out that no one, including judges, can accurately predict future human behavior.

I didn't agree then. I thought the judge was responsible for the death of those children. I feel differently now.

This case illustrates not only how difficult many of the cases are for a judge to decide, but also that there are many reasons that a judge's decision can turn out to be just plain wrong.

Lying Witnesses

If everyone told the truth, trials would move more quickly—and everyone would be happy with the results. But a sad truth is that witnesses who have sworn to tell the truth lie in court every day. And one of the reasons you may receive a decision that is wrong is that the judge may believe a witness who lies while testifying for your spouse. It's just another downside of the courtroom experience.

Because lying is an especially common problem in the charged atmosphere of a divorce trial, here are a few tips on what to do if you are forced to take your case to court and you are concerned about the possibility of your spouse fabricating damaging testimony.

- **Find out ahead of time what lies to expect.** Perhaps your spouse will tell you informally what evidence he or she plans to present in court. If not, there is a legal process called "discovery" that can be used to obtain that information. This is something that lawyers do regularly. It can be a little tricky to navigate on your own.

RESOURCES

If you decide to conduct your own discovery, the process is explained well in *Represent Yourself in Court,* by Paul Bergman and Sara J. Berman-Barrett (Nolo).

- **Gather documents or witnesses to present the truth in court.** As with the discovery process mentioned above, you may want to hire a lawyer for help with getting documents and testimony into evidence. For example, if there is a dispute about how your child is doing in school, serve a subpoena on the teacher to come to court and testify about it. If the disagreement involves some financial transactions, serve a subpoena on the financial agency involved so that the representative can verify what occurred. If you need an agency representative to bring records to court, you use something called a subpoena duces tecum, also explained in detail in the book mentioned above.

These procedures take some time to set up, so don't wait until the week before your hearing or trial to get them underway.

> ### Lies Usually Go Unpunished
>
> Strangely, even when the lies are clearly documented, the liars who tell them are rarely prosecuted. During my career on the bench, I reported three pretty outrageous lies to the district attorney's office, which never took any action on them.
>
> One of the lies involved a man who stole some stationery from a blood testing agency and manufactured a letter stating he was not the father of a child. The letter looked a little strange, so I called the agency, which recalled the man coming in and presenting a phony story about needing a piece of its letterhead. I had the man arrested and sent to jail. The district attorney didn't bring charges.
>
> But of course, the reluctant father lost his case—and was ordered to pay support for the child.

Disgruntled Judges

Given the importance of decisions in divorce cases, you might think that the most talented judges available would be assigned to hear them. You would be wrong.

Serving as a divorce judge is usually considered one of the least attractive judicial assignments around. Many judges end up presiding in a divorce court simply because they don't have enough seniority or other "juice" to claim a more prestigious spot doing civil jury trials or important criminal cases. Some count the months until they will be reassigned and let it be known they will do anything they can do to avoid a return assignment.

Because of the political process that results in most judges being elected or appointed to the bench, few lawyers who specialize in divorce law end up as judges. Unless they have been divorced themselves, many have had little reason to think about the process since the time they were forced to study it to pass the state bar examination.

The distaste many judges have for serving in divorce court is not difficult to understand. Family law judges have a saying: "In criminal courts, you deal with bad people on their best behavior. In family court, you deal with good people on their worst behavior." And there is quite a bit of truth to that saying. Many people in the process of divorce are going through one of the most difficult periods of their lives. Sometimes they say and do stupid—even despicable—things they would normally never think of saying or doing. Dealing every day with that sort of conduct can be depressing.

And it doesn't show signs of improving. One family law judge recently wrote to me about his experience in returning to the divorce court bench after a stint in retirement: "Upon my return, I found that the level of acrimony was even higher than it was when I left five years before. The concept of truth had totally disappeared with some litigants. They would say whatever they thought would put them in an advantageous position. The longer a judge stays in family law, the higher the stress levels become."

There are exceptions, though—divorce judges who look forward to each day as an opportunity "to do the right thing" for people in a difficult time. And a number of judges sent to serve in family court plunge right in, take courses to become familiar with the practicalities and the law, and are soon become extremely good at what they are doing.

However, the fact that there are a good number of judges who want to avoid being in family court is another reason you should avoid it yourself if possible.

When Justice Is Its Own Reward

In one of the most memorable trials of my career, I had to decide who would get custody of an eight-month-old baby orphaned by the devastating Loma Prieta earthquake in California in 1989.

The child, Jimmy, was destined to become a rich person after both of his parents were crushed to death in the collapse of part of a freeway. The state admitted there were errors in building what was the first double-decker freeway structure in California and offered to pay hundreds of thousands of dollars for survivors of those killed in the collapse.

Seeking guardianship of Jimmy were two sets of grandparents, other relatives, friends of his parents, and people from all over the country who learned about the child from newspapers and television news programs. Most of them made it clear that the money was of no concern to them—they just wanted to help a child who had become known in the press as "The Quake Orphan." Some of the relatives hired lawyers to pursue their cause. Others wrote beautiful letters in support.

With the help of the court staff, I reviewed the many applications and chose an impressive family who lived on a farm in the San Joaquin Valley with their child. The father of the family was related to Jimmy's mother.

When later asked by a reporter for the *New York Times* if I felt like King Solomon choosing among so many people to place this baby, I said: "No—although this is one of those wonderful opportunities to do the right thing, which is why you decide you want to be a judge."

Consider Alternatives to Divorce Court

The previous chapter should have at least caused you to question whether there isn't some better way to end your marriage than by going to divorce court.

Fortunately, there are at least three approaches that are clearly superior.

Reaching an agreement together. This involves you and your spouse sitting down and quietly reaching agreement on how your possessions and debts will be divided, whether one of you will pay the other support and how much—and if you have children, how they are going to be raised. (See "Working Out a Solution Together," below.) For some couples, reaching a settlement on these issues will be so easy that it can be accomplished in one meeting. For others, it makes sense to keep the stress level down by spreading the task out to several meetings.

Using mediation. Here, the two of you meet with a neutral person, called a mediator, who helps guide you through the process of reaching an agreement on possessions, debts, support, and child custody.

Most couples who use mediation locate their own mediator and participate in the process voluntarily.

However, some courts also have the power to order mediation—at least for some disputed issues in a divorce. For example, if the spouses do not reach an agreement between themselves, many courts in a number of states—including Arizona, California, Florida, Hawaii, Maine, Minnesota, Nevada, North Carolina, South Dakota, Utah, Washington, and Wisconsin—require them to meet with a court-appointed mediator on issues related to children such as custody, visitation, medical care, transportation, and schools. In many other states, a judge may order mediation if he or she thinks it's appropriate. And in a few states, the court's mediator can also help a couple settle disputes over finances and other issues. (See "Going to Mediation," below, for more detail on all divorce mediation procedures.)

Hiring collaborative lawyers. You and your spouse each choose an attorney who is specially trained in this rather new and growing method of divorcing. The lawyers who practice collaborative law call it "an alternative to divorce as usual." The process is based upon a written pledge from both spouses to reach an agreement on the terms of their divorce without going to court. They agree that if either party breaks that pledge by dragging the case into court, both attorneys must withdraw from the case and the spouses will be forced to hire new lawyers and start over again. It often works amazingly well, but is not yet available in all parts of the country. (See "Using Collaborative Law," below.)

Wisdom of the Ages

"Discourage litigation. Persuade your neighbors to compromise whenever you can. Point out to them how the nominal winner is often a real loser—in fees, expenses, and waste of time. As a peacemaker, the lawyer has a superior opportunity of being a good man. There will still be business enough."

Source: Abraham Lincoln, "Notes for a Law Lecture," *Life and Writing of Abraham Lincoln*, Modern Library, 2000

Advantages to the Alternatives

None of these alternative methods guarantees a harmonious divorce, but if you and your spouse commit to proceeding with one of these approaches and follow it in good faith, you are almost sure to avoid the terrible wear and tear of divorce court. In the process, you will also get a solution you can both live with more easily—and save yourselves quite a bit of time and money.

Reaching a Fitting Solution

Going to court means you will have a trial in a public courtroom where the goal is to find a result that the judge thinks is appropriate. Bear in mind that a judge, who will have only limited information about you and your spouse, may or may not have the time or interest in attempting to tailor the best possible resolution to your situation. And a judge's decree often produces unpredictable results that at least one of you will hate.

These alternatives to going to court all take place in a private setting in which the goal is to find an agreement acceptable to both of you. After all, you and your spouse know best the intricacies of the relationship you have developed during your marriage. And there probably will be no opportunity for anyone to testify in a trial about why "it is only fair" that one or the other of you should be awarded an object of art, the convertible car, or the family dog. The judge may find it irrelevant that late one night, you both agreed that when one of you got a college degree, the other one would be entitled to finish the required courses for a teaching credential. And the judge will never meet your child and form a personal opinion about the most fitting custody or visitation arrangement.

Saving Time

One of the worst aspects of the court system is that it gobbles up huge amounts of time for divorcing spouses—and for any lawyers they may have hired to represent them. The major reason is that the administrators who run the courts have goals similar to those of most business managers: They want to make the most efficient possible use of their employees. Having judges and courtroom staff sitting around waiting for the next case to arrive is not efficient. So the administrators schedule more cases than can possibly be handled at various hours of the day. They know that some of these cases will be settled in the hallway outside of the courtroom. Others will be continued over to a future day because of conflicts in lawyer's schedules, sickness, car problems, or some other unpredictable cause.

As a result of all this, the court may schedule 30 cases for a session beginning at 9 a.m. On most days, at least 20 of those cases will be settled the day before or out in the hallway on the morning of the hearing. Perhaps only ten of them will actually require a hearing—and every one of those will likely get heard. But every once in a while, most of the people involved in all 30 cases will show up and require a hearing before the same judge. Some will involve emergency issues that will get priority attention.

It is not unusual for attorneys involved in a case to arrive in the courtroom and announce: "If we can have just a few minutes with the judge in chambers, we think we can reach a total settlement of the whole case today." The prospect of settling a case will woo some judges off the bench and into chambers for what is often more time than was predicted. When the noon recess arrives, cases that have not been heard that day usually are postponed to another time. Sometimes the calendars are so jammed, it will be a month or more before a new date is available. For this and other reasons, taking your case to court involves a lot of sitting in the audience and wasting time.

But even if you get lucky and are heard promptly in court at the assigned time on the scheduled day, the number of times you can be forced to come back to court to fight over relatively insignificant matters can stretch into hundreds of hours if either you or your spouse are determined to carry on a battle over every issue.

The bigger point here is that once you have filed an action for divorce in court, you lose control over how long the case may keep you embroiled in the process. Disputes over obtaining information through the discovery process, applications for changes in support or custody rulings, and appeals can force you to stay tied to your old marriage for years. And the time you spend waiting in a courtroom for the judge to hear your case can run into seemingly endless hours.

The Long Goodbye

One of the most wasteful cases I have been connected with involved two lawyers who represented themselves. I was assigned to their case after my retirement because the judges in the county where the case was pending all either disqualified themselves or were removed by a challenge filed by one of the parties.

The only reason the parties didn't battle over child support or custody was because they had no children. And they didn't battle over alimony because they had similar earning abilities and their marriage had lasted just barely two years. Their debts exceeded their assets, so dividing their possessions should not have been terribly complicated.

During the course of litigation, they filed 16 requests for review in the state court of appeal and at least two in the state's supreme court.

Most of their battling involved a small two-story office building in the small Northern California town where both of them practiced law. One spouse went through the other's garbage cans looking for evidence to prove that there were earnings that were not reported to the court.

In a 2006 hearing, the wife of the couple asked to be allowed to appear by telephone because of her fear for her life if she returned to the county seat, where the hearing would be held. In several of the appellate rulings, the court pointed out that "the parties have allowed this litigation to get totally out of hand, a waste not only of their time and money but a major imposition on court resources."

The papers they have filed in the trial court fill more than 30 volumes. One of the parties served five days in the county jail for contempt of court. Both of them have now filed actions in bankruptcy court. And their case continues unresolved, nearly 12 years after it was filed.

Saving Money

The financial benefit to staying out of court is probably obvious. Trial lawyers charge for their time by the hour, whether they are waiting in the courtroom or cross-examining a witness on the stand. The three alternatives discussed in this chapter involve almost no waiting time—and involve little or no time from lawyers. They also avoid many of the time-consuming paper shuffling used in the law to subpoena documents, take depositions, and argue over what are often silly legal issues. The parties involved or their lawyers produce the necessary documents, and everyone's time is used in working out a solution rather than litigating.

> ⚠ **WARNING**
> **The high cost of going to court.** I have handled more than a dozen cases where lawyer fees for each side were more than $100,000. And I have seen very few where a lawyer charged less than $1,000 for a contested divorce. In most contested cases, fees will be at least $10,000.

When Alternative Methods May Not Work

Unfortunately, there are situations in which the alternatives to court discussed here may not work. Many people really seem doomed to divorce the ugly way: in court.

There are a number of scenarios that may fit that category—including when your spouse hires combative counsel or when he or she is a bully, uncommunicative, missing, or lacks good faith.

> ⇨ **SKIP AHEAD**
> If none of these unfortunate situations applies to you, skip ahead to "A look at the Alternatives," below.

Combative Counsel Is Involved

It can be difficult to resolve your divorce out of court if one spouse has fallen under the spell of an aggressive lawyer—sometimes known as "a Bomber"—who has convinced him or her that mediation and collaborative law is sissy stuff that will fail to produce any agreement, anyway. Or, if there is an agreement, the lawyer might argue that it won't be as good as he or she could get in court. Some lawyers of this variety brag about how much they will enjoy "chewing up" the other party on the witness stand.

If your spouse hires a lawyer like this—common if he or she is angry and wants to use the divorce as a way of obtaining revenge—you are at high risk of spending loads of expensive, comparatively unproductive time in court.

What you can do: This may be a good time to try circumventing the lawyer's pull and to get more actively involved in resolving disputes on your own. *Divorce Without Court: A Guide to Mediation & Collaborative Divorce,* by Katherine E. Stoner (Nolo), contains an excellent plan for proposing mediation to a spouse—including a discussion of when mediation should be suggested, different methods of making the proposal, and how your spouse's degree of anger or sadness may affect an agreement to mediate.

Finding a trusted friend or relative to talk to your spouse about avoiding unnecessary conflict can also be effective.

Where the Knowing Fear to Tread

When a friend recently asked me to provide some advice on who he should hire as his divorce lawyer, I gave him a list of several experienced lawyers. He talked to them all and then reported back that none would take the case when he revealed to them who his wife's lawyer was.

The reason they gave was simple: They don't take cases in which they knew the opposing lawyer was a "Bomber," because they require so much time playing legal games over inconsequential matters. It was stressful for the lawyer and embarrassingly expensive for the client. They recommended talking to a younger and less experienced lawyer who might enjoy the exercise.

Your Spouse Is a Bully

It can also be tough to proceed with an alternative to divorce court if your spouse has a history of intimidating and abusing you so that as a matter of self-preservation, you have given up and "lost" almost all of the arguments that have taken place during your marriage.

Attempting to negotiate on your own can be a waste of time in this situation. Your spouse is probably so used to winning all of your arguments that he or she will insist on unreasonable terms for the divorce and refuse to negotiate meaningfully.

There are some skilled mediators who can overcome this hurdle—particularly those who have had a lot of experience in the courtroom and can explain to your spouse with some authority what is likely to happen if settlement isn't possible and the case goes to trial. Unfortunately, however, many seasoned bullies will avoid mediation, fearing that a calm and objective airing of the dispute will cause them to lose the upper hand at intimidation.

What you can do: If your spouse is a reasonably frugal sort who is made to understand that a full-blown fight in court is sure to be long and expensive, there may also be some hope in changing his or her direction. Point out the costly personal and financial aspects of a contested divorce for each of you, for any children who may be involved, and for your extended families. Make it clear you are not proposing any particular settlement of the divorce; you simply want to resolve it peacefully.

Ministers, priests, and spiritual advisers are often very skilled in helping in a situation such as this. Buying your spouse a copy of *Divorce Without Court: A Guide to Mediation & Collaborative Divorce,* by Katherine E. Stoner (Nolo), could also be a good investment.

Your Spouse Is Uncommunicative

Some spouses won't cooperate in talking reasonably about the terms of a divorce. If your spouse hesitates in this way, perhaps the reason is that he or she has not contacted a lawyer yet—or, even worse, has found one of the "Bomber" lawyers described above and can't wait to see you "chewed up" in court.

Some spouses clam up or lash out because they are so angry about the reality of a divorce. Others are too hurt. Some just plain refuse to talk about it at all. And there are those who just want to rant and rave about how ungrateful you are and how they are going to "take you to the cleaners"—and so on and so on. The bottom line is that such hurt and angry people refuse to communicate meaningfully.

What you can do: If you have worn out all possible lines of communication, the only thing you can do is to file an action for divorce in your local court and have your spouse served with the relevant papers. After such spouses read over the summons and see the penalties for ignoring the legal proceeding, they are often more likely to want to talk, or to hire a lawyer to talk for them. That can open up all the possibilities discussed in this chapter.

Your Spouse Is Missing

Obviously, if your spouse has left town, it may be impossible to have a constructive conversation with him or her about how to end your marriage. In fact, there are a surprising number of cases in which a spouse who claims to be dashing down to the corner to buy a pack of cigarettes never comes back.

If this, or something like it, is your situation, you probably will eventually be able to obtain a judgment declaring the marriage terminated—also called "dissolved" in many states—without ever locating your spouse.

What you can do: For a number of reasons, discussed below, it is likely to be worth your while to do a bit of footwork to discover where your spouse might be located and served with divorce papers. This could be as simple and inexpensive as calling old friends, relatives, or employers who might know his or her whereabouts. And it could be as complicated and expensive as hiring a private detective to do the finding for you.

Most states provide a mechanism for serving a missing spouse who can't be found by publishing a legal notice in a newspaper (which your spouse will almost certainly never read) or posting a notice on a courthouse bulletin board (which he or she will most likely never see). If your court has a general divorce advice service or facilitator, you may be able to get instructions there on how to follow the required publication process. You will normally be required to file a sworn statement reporting how you lost contact with your spouse and verifying that you checked with former employers, relatives, the Department of Motor Vehicles, and the post office to try to find him or her.

The local court clerk's office may be able to give you some help, but you also may find that this area is a little too technical for the staffers there. If you planned to do your divorce without having a lawyer and all of the leads to finding your spouse fail, consider hiring an attorney who specializes in family law to help you through just this portion of your case. (See "Unbundling Legal Services" in Chapter 5 for help in finding a fitting lawyer.)

To be successful in this sort of a situation, you will probably have to convince a judge that even after you made a diligent try, your spouse really couldn't be found. Even if you succeed in this, the only thing you can be sure of having settled for all time is the fact that the marriage has been terminated and that you are single again.

The other possible terms of the judgment about child custody and visitation, support, and division of your possessions are not as secure as if you had actually served the papers on your spouse. The reason for this is that the law is loathe to enforce an order against a person who had no real opportunity to argue about how much support he or she should have to pay or why he or she shouldn't be allowed to visit the children on their birthdays.

Also, the truth is that few very people actually comply with a judgment that is obtained by publication. Human nature is such that people are more likely to obey an order that resulted from a hearing for which they received notice, or better yet, one in which they personally participated.

Your Spouse Lacks Good Faith

It doesn't happen often, but in some cases, one of the spouses attempts to hide a substantial asset or take some other dishonest action during the course of a divorce. (See Chapter 6, When Dividing Your Property, Don't Hide the Ball.)

Such bad behavior often stems from a spouse who:

• hates the other so much that he or she will tell any lie, conceal any asset, and poison any well available

• is having an affair with a new lover, especially when that paramour has experience in business and finance

• is so surprised and injured by the idea of a divorce that all he or she can think of is getting revenge, or

• is so fixated on acquiring wealth that he or she will do almost anything for a few more dollars.

What you can do. If you think your spouse may fit into this category, your first step should be to gather every financial record you can find, make copies, and get them out of the house and into a secure place.

Past income tax returns may often contain especially valuable clues leading to assets you didn't know existed. If, for instance, the tax return indicates that interest is being paid on some asset, it may reveal that something has been hidden. And if you can't locate all of the pages of a particular joint tax return, or if you suspect that the copy your spouse gives you is not the same one you jointly sent in to the government, you should be able to obtain a copy from the Internal Revenue Service.

If you have access to a computer your spouse uses in your home, you may be able to copy the files to examine and analyze later. But be aware that this is a situation in which it will be particularly valuable for you to be represented by a lawyer or forensic accountant who has had some experience in finding hidden assets.

Lawyers: To Hire or Not to Hire

Some people are clear about whether or not they intend to hire a lawyer for help nearly from their first thought about splitting. For others, it is still an open question. (See "Hiring a Lawyer" in Chapter 5 for advice on finding and choosing one.) However, it is important to consider the possibility even if you want to attempt to settle your divorce directly with your spouse or through mediation.

If the financial facts of your situation are very clear and simple, it may be perfectly appropriate to attempt to work things out on your own or with the help of a mediator. However, if you are determined not to hire a lawyer and you have joint accounts, some fairly large bills, income tax problems, or retirement plans or stock options to be dealt with, it is wise to do a little homework before you get started. A quick and easy way to get educated is to read *Divorce & Money: How to Make the Best Financial Decisions During Divorce,* by Violet Woodhouse and Dale Fetherling (Nolo). You can pick and choose the subjects in the book that apply to your situation, but you definitely should do at least that. It is very possible that what you learn will have a serious affect on what you agree to in any settlement.

In fact, educating yourself about the financial facts of divorce is a good idea even if you are going to use a lawyer to help through the process. And if you opt to mediate, the mediator may also give both of you advice on financial matters. However, before relying on such advice, be sure you know what training and experience he or she has in this field.

A Look at the Alternatives

If you have steered around all of the perils listed above, it is time to consider how you might use the alternatives mentioned at the beginning of this chapter. Except in an unusual case, it is my serious and experienced advice that the courtroom is not the best place for you to resolve the details of your divorce.

Working Out a Solution Together

Although it is not the stuff of television soap operas, there are a great number of divorcing couples who can actually agree on some or all the terms of their divorce while sitting down together around the kitchen table or other spot and hashing them out together.

They typically include:

- younger couples in short marriages with no children, where both partners feel they have made a mistake in getting married
- couples in midlife who have stayed together "for the children"—and whose children are now grown
- spouses whose lives have taken such divergent turns into new career or areas of interest that they now have little in common, and
- reasonable people of all ages and stages.

The two necessary characteristics of these couples are reasonableness and a clear respect for one another. One or both of the spouses may feel they will be happier living by themselves or with a new partner, but they want to accomplish their divorce in a fair and trusting way.

Those on the outside looking in—particularly professionals who make their money from the business of divorcing—often decry this sensible scenario in dire tones.

"Oh, no," say some lawyers. "They probably won't know about the new law the legislature just passed about spousal support. They shouldn't bargain without a lawyer at their elbows."

"That's very dangerous," claim many certified public accountants and tax advisors. "They should have an audit of their financial situation and an appraisal of the assets. Without that, they are at a big risk of creating problems that could cost them a lot in unnecessary taxes."

Despite these warnings, I have signed off on thousands of divorces in which couples have agreed to a very reasonable settlement without the help of lawyers or accountants. Some of them involved fairly substantial assets. When I have asked the couples whether they had considered new laws or the tax consequences of their agreement, many have just smiled and asked that I simply approve what they had agreed to between themselves.

Tips for the Settlement Talk

If you and your spouse are still speaking to one another in a halfway friendly manner, it is a good idea to try to work things out together—at least initially. Start with the understanding that this is just a nonbinding attempt to see if you can save some aggravation. And both of you should understand that if you have children, you are giving them a wonderful gift if you are able to keep things amicable.

There are a few steps you can follow to help make these discussions more focused and productive.

Make a list of all of your possessions and see if you can agree who should get what. (See "Dividing Your Own Property" in Chapter 6 for more on this.) Write down a list of the things you own together and agree to review it together in a few days when you have both had time to think it over. Do the same thing with your debts.

ADDITIONAL RESOURCES

For those who need more help, *Divorce & Money: How to Make the Best Financial Decisions During Divorce,* by Violet Woodhouse and Dale Fetherling (Nolo), includes guidance for divorcing couples who are considering and listing property and expenses.

If you have children, try to work out a schedule for times they will spend with each parent. In some cases, you may even feel comfortable talking directly with the children about some possible custody plans. Write down the possibilities and go over them again with your spouse after a few days. In many situations, it will be a good idea to attempt to make a plan now for just the next six months. If that appeals to you, provide in your agreement that the two of you will meet again on a certain date to see how your custody plan has been working and to make warranted changes

Try to figure out what it is going to cost each of you to live separately. Do this by writing down a list of expenses: rent, utilities, groceries, insurance, transportation. Take a look at what your tax returns indicate each of your yearly incomes have been and what they are likely to be in the near future. Consider whether and how your joint incomes can support these new separate lifestyles.

Consider the possibility of paying and receiving support or alimony. If the issues are going to be part of your settlement, carefully read Chapter 7 on alimony and Chapter 8 on child support and see if you can reach some agreement on what these amounts should be and for how long they should be paid. Keep in mind that alimony is tax-deductible by the one who pays and taxable to the one who receives it. Child support is neither deductible nor taxable by either person.

Finalizing Your Agreement

Once you and your spouse have agreed on the major terms of your divorce, you have two choices of what to do next.

Handling simple agreements on your own. The simplest approach is to write down all the terms of your agreement. Then ask the local court to set the case for trial and when that date arrives, give the judge a copy of your agreement to incorporate into your judgment of divorce.

Some judges will accept your agreement even though it isn't typed up as a formal legal document. If it isn't too long, they will simply read it into the court's record where it is taken down by a court reporter or electronically recorded.

Most judges will appreciate the fact that you are simplifying the court's work on a case that otherwise would have had to been scheduled for a trial. Other judges may not be so eager to do this and insist that you get your joint understanding translated into a more formal format.

To get started, ask the court clerk's office for the form to request a trial date. If the form requires you to estimate how long your trial will take, indicate "ten minutes." Hopefully, this will save you from having to put your kitchen table agreement into more formal legal format, called a Marital Settlement Agreement, as discussed below. However, before it is all over, you probably are still going to have draft at least one more document called a judgment after the trial. Some paralegals may be able to help do this inexpensively. (See "Independent Paralegals" in Chapter 5 for details on this.)

Having Your Agreement Reviewed by a Lawyer

If you haven't talked to a lawyer before reaching a written agreement, it often is a good idea to have any tentative agreement reviewed by a lawyer who is knowledgeable in divorce law. This is true except in the very simplest divorce in a short marriage.

It is very possible the parties will forget an important issue that should be resolved before they go their separate ways. For example, have they dealt with providing health insurance for the children? Have they considered what will happen to a house they own jointly if one spouse dies? Sometimes there are tax or pension issues that should be investigated. Having an expert review issues such as this is almost always a good idea.

Chapter 5 provides thorough advice on how to choose a lawyer. But in the situation discussed here, note that when you make your initial call to a lawyer, you should be clear that one or both of you want to meet to review an agreement you have already reached. If this is the kind of a service the lawyer accepts, let him or her know at the beginning of your meeting that the major decisions are pretty well settled and that you just want to be alerted to any problems the two of you may have missed.

Some lawyers are concerned about possible conflicts of interest and do not want to accept assignments to meet with both parties to process their divorce agreement. However, many states now have rules for lawyers that make such an arrangement appropriate if the lawyer explains that he or she is not representing either of the parties individually and is not responsible for adverse circumstances that may result. The lawyer will have both spouses sign a written statement that they understand this and agree to it. (See "Unbundled Legal Services" in Chapter 5 for more on these arrangements.)

Of course, if you'd feel more comfortable, you can have individual lawyers review the agreement for each of you separately. Lawyers hired to do this are much more likely to be nitpicky and combative than an individual working for both of you.

Getting help with a Marital Settlement Agreement. If you don't want to handle finalizing your agreement yourself, another option is to hire a lawyer or paralegal to turn your agreement into a Marital Settlement Agreement and to submit it to the court. This approach will probably enable you to become divorced much sooner than under the first procedure, but it could set you back at least a few hundred dollars.

A Marital Settlement Agreement, or MSA, is not legally required, but is almost always drafted by a lawyer in cases that involve assets with medium to high value. An MSA, which can run from three to 30 or more pages long, must be signed by both parties and any lawyers involved. It will list the couple's possessions and who will own what, how much support will be paid between them, and how long such payments will continue.

MSAs often include a lot of recitations about when the parties were married, when they separated, and the names and birth dates of any children. And if there are children, the agreements usually will specify where they shall live and when they shall visit each of their parents, as well as who will pay for their educations.

An MSA can provide for insurance that one will take out on the life of the other in the event the spouse paying support dies while child support or alimony is still being paid. It also may include details such as what happens if the IRS audits a tax return that has been filed in the past, and what is to happen if the couple decides to reconcile sometime in the future. And it may also include provisions for eventualities that are even more unlikely than that.

When it has been all typed up and signed by the parties and their lawyers, it is presented to the court for incorporation in a judgment of divorce. If the parties have reached a Marital Settlement Agreement, in many counties, it isn't necessary for either of them to even appear in a courtroom. Their divorce can all be handled by mail. As mentioned, a lawyer will normally charge several hundred dollars to draft such an agreement.

Going to Mediation

If you and your spouse were not able to reach an agreement together or one of you feels that the situation is just too fraught with problems to work out without outside help, your next stop might well be mediation.

Understanding the Process

A divorce mediator is a person who, usually in exchange for an hourly fee, meets with a divorcing couple to help them reach an agreement on some or all of the terms of their divorce. Don't confuse mediation—as many people do—with arbitration, which is a more formal procedure quite similar to going to court. An arbitrator has the power and duty to decide how a dispute will be resolved. Arbitration is rarely used in divorce situations.

A mediator has no legal power to force you to do anything, just skill and training in helping people reach an agreement. He or she sets and enforces some ground rules and makes sure that each party is treated respectfully. It is also the mediator's job to make sure the parties talk through the decisions they make and listen to one another while working out an agreement together. In mediation, sometimes spouses choose to be represented by lawyers, either in the meetings with the mediator, or afterward when a tentative agreement has been reached.

If you wish, you are totally free to quit and walk out of a mediation meeting at any time; the proceedings are entirely voluntary. That isn't true of divorce courts. Most courtrooms are staffed with a bailiff who, if the judge directs, will sit you down to at least listen to your trial.

Mediations usually take place at the mediator's office and may take several sessions. Unlike a court trial in which each party's testimony is limited by the rules of evidence, everyone in a mediation is encouraged to share their thoughts about the divorce without interruption.

Your first meeting with a mediator will usually begin with an explanation of the mediation process, the confidentiality of what takes place in your sessions, and the expectation that you will achieve the goal of reaching a written agreement settling the issues of your divorce. The mediator will probably explain that it is your role to make the decisions—and that his or her role is to help you find acceptable compromises, not to act as a judge or decision maker.

If you and your spouse agree to proceed with mediation, the mediator may ask you both to sign a written agreement to mediate. It will usually include provisions underscoring that you both agree to abide by established guidelines for the process, that the mediation talks are confidential—and explaining how you will be charged for the mediator's services.

At this juncture, the mediator may ask you and your spouse to identify issues to be resolved. These may include:

• Who is to get the house—or is it to be sold?

• How are your other possessions and investments to be divided?

• If there are children, how will their time be split between the parents and what child support should be paid?

• Will there be alimony—and, if so, how much and for how long will it be paid?

In most cases, a second meeting will be scheduled, to which you probably will be asked to bring along a number of financial documents and past income tax returns. You will be urged to talk honestly about what you want to achieve in a settlement and to express your fears and frustrations. There may be rules about personal conduct during the sessions, but even emotional expressions about the issues are frequently helpful and sometimes encouraged by the mediator so that one spouse understands just how important an issue is to the other spouse.

The next tasks will be to identify where the parties agree and disagree and to negotiate solutions. Mediators all work differently in this discussion phase; some will hold separate sessions with just one spouse and shuttle back and forth between two rooms. Others believe firmly that everything should be done in joint sessions.

It is often necessary to hold a number of mediation sessions, providing time for the parties to consult with advisors and think privately about possible compromises to which they would agree. If the mediation is successful—and sometimes they are not—a written Marital Settlement Agreement is prepared and must then be taken to court to be incorporated into a divorce judgment.

> ⚠ **WARNING**
> **Domestic violence may complicate mediation.** Using mediation in divorce cases in which domestic violence has occurred is somewhat controversial. Many argue that because of the fear engendered by the violence, there is the likelihood of an imbalance of power and that therefore mediation should never be used. Others argue that if the problem is addressed and procedural safeguards provided, mediation can proceed as long as the person who may have suffered abuse or violence feels comfortable. If you are in this situation, be sure to be up front about any hesitancy or fear you feel. (See "Dealing With Domestic Violence" in Chapter 10 for information on how to get help if your spouse is threatening or otherwise abusing you.)

Finding a Mediator

All sorts of people work in what probably should be called the art of mediation. Many have tremendously successful records of obtaining a fair agreement. There are also some who have had no particular education in the field and just decided to hang out a shingle and start mediating.

This section of the chapter includes an explanation of the major players and groups—and a bit about them to help you assess who might be a good fit for your situation. In the final analysis, you want a mediator with whom you feel comfortable and one who has a good reputation with other professionals in your community. If there are major financial issues, you want someone who can demonstrate experience in this area. If child custody is a major issue, an accountant is probably not your best choice. Inquire around—and importantly, talk with prospective candidates before making a hiring decision.

Lawyer/mediators. There are some lawyers in almost every community who mediate divorce agreements. Many lawyers don't have extensive training in the dynamics of personal counseling and the techniques of mediation, but some have a personality that uniquely lends itself to resolving disputes. One advantage that a seasoned divorce lawyer/mediator may offer is knowledge about legal and tax complications that may be involved in your situation. A disadvantage with some lawyers is that they will attempt to steer you toward a settlement that they think is right for you, rather than something that is more aligned with your unique situation.

Lawyer/mediators are typically more expensive than mediators who do not have law degrees—generally charging between $200 and $400 an hour for their services. Still, even if a divorce mediation takes several days, this is a bargain compared to the costly alternative of litigating.

Marriage and family counselors. Many states license counselors, and a person having such a license is very likely to have specific training and experience in divorce mediation. Because most counselors are not lawyers, they do not draw up the formal Marital Settlement Agreement that a lawyer/mediator would prepare, but normally put the matters agreed upon in a memorandum that will provide the parties or a lawyer with the information necessary to prepare a more formal agreement. Counselors' hourly rates tend to be quite a bit lower than lawyers' rates, normally less than $200 an hour.

Other individuals. Other people, for example, psychologists and clergy, also engage in mediation. As long as they have specialized training in the discipline—and the temperament and patience to listen—they can be very fine mediators. The rates they charge vary widely and the way to find the best may be through family, friends, and associates who have had a good experience with a particular individual.

Community groups. Many communities have agencies that provide mediation at a very reasonable fee—often $30 or less an hour. Their mediators may be paid or possibly work as volunteers. Most have had mediation training and some work for the agency to obtain the experience that will eventually allow them to open their own practices.

It may take a little scouting around to find out if there is a community mediation group that handles divorce in your area. If your state has a Department of Consumer Affairs, its website will probably contain contacts to available resources. County Departments of Social Services can be helpful, as can legal aid societies and county bar associations, which frequently make referrals to nonlawyer resources for people with limited incomes.

Court-annexed mediation. A growing number of courts offer some form of mediation. However, many of these court programs only deal with the subject of sharing custody of children. Some have a compulsory orientation program and offer a short mediation without charge. If you don't see a sign or brochure in the clerk's office of your local family court, ask one of the clerks at the counter whether the court has such a program. You can also call the local court or consult its website for more information.

If your court requires that parties participate in mediation, you will be informed of this when your case is first filed with the court. Normally this service will not be available before then.

Court programs differ as to whether there are full-time professional mediators working as court employees or whether they refer couples out to private mediators or volunteers with varying amounts of experience. If you have a lawyer, he or she will know the advantages and disadvantages of each alternative.

Retired judges. Retired judges are available as mediators through local mediation services and several nationwide organizations. Their hourly fees are usually in the range of $300 to $500 an hour, thus limiting their availability to a fairly small group of divorcing couples.

The advantage of using former judges is that their predictions of how a court will decide a particular issue if the parties don't settle is usually well-informed and accurate.

The disadvantage is that some of them are stuck in their ways and may be more comfortable ruling on their own as they have in the past rather than listening to the parties and encouraging them to fashion their own settlements. Local bar associations normally can make referrals to retired judges who mediate. Local lawyers tend to be very familiar with the records of judges and can guide their clients in a specific choice.

A Lost Mediating Opportunity

Mediation often makes it possible for divorcing spouses to avoid the aggressive parts of going to court that only serve to drive them further apart and make settlement impossible.

For example, I was recently the judge in a case in which the wife's parents had given the couple almost $100,000 toward purchasing their first home when the couple married. Eight years later, they were having an angry divorce. We spent two days trying the issue of whether the parents had intended for the money to be a gift or a loan, and, if it was a gift, whether they intended to be given to the wife alone or to the couple.

One of the exhibits introduced in evidence was a gift card that came with the check from the parents on the wedding day. The parties wouldn't even agree whether the card was real or a fake.

By the time the case was over, the couple had spent more than $10,000 litigating and both camps were refusing to exchange even a glance across the courtroom.

After I announced my decision, one of the lawyers admitted that a few minutes before the trial started, they were only a few thousand dollars short of a settlement, but that nobody would budge another dollar. I honestly believe that if they had hired an adept mediator, they could have neatly settled their differences.

ADDITIONAL RESOURCE

For more on divorce mediation, see *Divorce Without Court: A Guide to Mediation & Collaborative Divorce*, by Katherine E. Stoner (Nolo). The book explains how to propose mediation to your spouse, find the right mediator, and handle everything from the first session to writing up your agreement. *A Guide to Divorce Mediation*, by Gary J. Friedman (Workman Publishing), is also an excellent guide displaying a detailed examination of many sample mediations.

Using Collaborative Law

Collaborative law is a relatively new and often successful way to stay out of court while getting divorced. It is designed for people who are so committed to settling a divorce out of court that they agree to pay a penalty if the case doesn't settle and they are forced to fall back to the court system.

Collaborative law works this way: Each spouse is represented by a specially trained lawyer whose only job is to negotiate a settlement that meets the legitimate needs of both parties. Each spouse is required to sign a binding agreement not to file any papers that would result in taking the case to court and not to threaten to do so. If either spouse violates that agreement, the collaborative process ends. The lawyers involved also agree that if, after numerous sessions, no settlement is reached, they will withdraw.

If you haven't had a lot of experience in the divorce business, the penalty may not seem obvious. Part of it is that the client loses a lawyer who has worked on the case for months *and* that a new attorney will have to be retained. Losing a lawyer who is familiar with the details of the case is a serious blow to most litigants. Finding a substitute lawyer and educating him or her on all that has gone on will cost at least $5,000 in a relatively simple case. And it will cost many, many times that in a more complex case.

In collaborative law, settlements are negotiated in meetings attended by each of the spouses and his or her lawyer. Sometimes experts on financial or custody matters join in to give their advice. After a session has terminated, the lawyers may continue to negotiate, checking back with their clients on new avenues that might be explored. Experienced lawyers can usually inform their clients what a probable result will be if the case is forced to go back into court. They concentrate their efforts in finding solutions, not engaging in all of the expensive legal maneuvers that are often part of a divorce litigated in the courtroom. Once an agreement has been reached, they prepare a Marital Settlement Agreement and present it to the court to approve and incorporate into a judgment of divorce.

More than 5,000 U.S. lawyers have been trained in the protocol of collaborative divorce. There are currently collaborative practitioners in every state except Alabama, Arkansas, Iowa, Montana, Nebraska, North Dakota, South Dakota, Tennessee, West Virginia, and Wyoming— although the popularity of the practice is growing daily. Check the website at www.collaborativedivorce.com for current local availability.

ADDITIONAL RESOURCE
For additional information on collaborative law, see *Collaborative Divorce: The Revolutionary New Way to Restructure Your Family, Resolve Legal Issues, and Move on With Your Life,* by Pauline Tesler and Peggy Thompson (Regan Books/Harper Collins).

WARNING
The gander is entitled to what's good for the goose. If you hire a collaborative lawyer and your spouse hires a lawyer who has not had collaborative training, some collaborative lawyers would not continue to represent you. Others would discuss the case with the other lawyer and may agree to proceed if he or she will agree to abide by collaborative rules for the individual case.

If You Must Go to Court, Follow These Tips

A s you learned in Chapter 1, the wisest approach is to do everything possible to handle your divorce without showing your face in a courtroom. But, because of the particular facts of your situation, it may not be possible for you to totally avoid that bewildering arena.

For example, you have no reasonable alternative but to go to court if:

• you and your spouse can't resolve all of the issues in your divorce and for some reason, mediation or collaborative divorce doesn't work

• your spouse won't pay court-ordered support, doesn't follow the schedule for visiting with your child, or gets physically or emotionally abusive with you (see Chapter 10 for more on handling these problems legally), or

• after a court has entered a judgment, circumstances change—such as you lose your job—and it is necessary to modify an existing court order.

So, with my hope that you never need to use them, this chapter contains a few tips on how to make any necessary court appearance as smooth and free from stress as possible.

(!) **WARNING**

When to ignore the advice in this book. This chapter is mostly for people who have not hired a lawyer to help with or completely handle their divorces. If you do have a lawyer, listen to him or her, not to the advice you read here. An experienced lawyer will have been down the divorce court path many times before and should know how to get the best result from your particular judge. If this book alerts you to something your lawyer hasn't covered, ask if he or she agrees with the advice here. If not, follow your lawyer's advice, not mine.

You may be wondering why it's necessary for you to pay attention to tips on how to handle yourself in court. After all, a court appearance simply requires you to get a few pieces of information to a judge so that he or she can make some relevant decisions.

That is true. But in an average day of judging in divorce court, I made 957 or more decisions. Some of them were on small matters, such as who should get the car that two spouses owned together. And some were on big ones—such as where the kids should spend Christmas, or how many hundreds of dollars per month one spouse would have to pay the other for child support or alimony. Those decisions were based on the law and on the particular facts or evidence in a case: for example, if one spouse worked in a dangerous part of town, it seemed logical that he or she should be awarded their car just for the sake of safety.

Like other divorce court judges, I tried to disregard things that were irrelevant—such as the fact that one spouse's new love was sitting in the front row of the courtroom carrying on like some kind of cheerleader. I might have glared at the cheerleader. I might even have asked the bailiff to escort him or her out of the courtroom. But when it came time to make a decision, I tried very hard to be sure something like that did not influence me. However, if you put me under oath and asked whether personal feelings had any influence on any ruling I ever made, I'd be hard pressed to say they never did.

As a more subtle example, judges should also apply tunnel vision to the person who walks into a courtroom in session, sits down in the front row of the audience section, starts wildly chewing some substance, and then pulls out a newspaper and flips through the pages. But such behavior would likely bother most judges on some level, because it shows disrespect for the institution in which important decisions are made and disrupts the dignified atmosphere.

Failing to show respect for the court and its standards of personal conduct may only detract slightly from how a judge evaluates your case. But a slight detraction can be decisive if your case presents a close call on who is to be believed.

This chapter offers tips on how you can help make sure that your conduct in court—or that of your friend in the front row—doesn't result in you losing a much needed point or two when the judge is, in effect, mentally adding up the scores for you and your spouse.

Throwing the Baby Out With the Custody Bid

Over the years, I've seen quite a few people who allowed their emotions to ruin their chances of winning in court. The worst case involved a custody battle over a baby who was about six months old. The mother and the father were both representing themselves in court without lawyers.

As the hearing began, the father walked up from the back of the courtroom with the baby girl wrapped in a blanket in his arms. As the testimony developed, it became clear that the father had picked up the child from a babysitter during the time she was supposed to be in the custody of the mother. He had decided that he was going to keep the baby until he and his wife "got some other things straightened out."

"No, you're not," I said, "I want you to hand that baby to her right now." And before anyone knew what happened, he turned and threw the baby 15 feet to a friend standing in the back of the courtroom. The mother screamed, the baby began to wail, and the bailiff ran to the back of the courtroom. I flipped the panic button under the bench, which is designed to bring hot and cold running sheriff's deputies from a squad room across the street.

By the time things had been calmed down, the father was in handcuffs and seemed to realize he had pretty well blown any chance he had of gaining custody of the child.

Different Scenarios: Motions and Trials

There are two types of legal actions that may bring your case into court: motions and trials.

Motions can be made either before or after a trial. Motions before a trial are usually made by a party to obtain the security of a court order that will govern some aspect of the parties' relations until the time of trial, as described below. Motions after trial are made to modify or enforce the orders already in place.

The trial itself is normally the most important event in the case and, depending on its complexity, may last anywhere from ten minutes to several months. After hearing the evidence produced by the parties at trial, the judge will decide any issues the parties have not been able to resolve on their own.

Pretrial Motions

Many divorces involve issues that require at least a temporary resolution between the time the case is filed and a trial is held. If you and your spouse agree on all of the short range issues listed below, there won't be any pretrial motions. If you don't agree and need some action before the court is ready to give you a trial, either one of you can file a motion to get what is usually an order that will only last until the time of total settlement or trial.

Pretrial motions are used to resolve a number of issues, including:

- money—how much one spouse should be required to pay to the other for child support or alimony pending the trial

- custody—how much time children should spend with each of the parents, where they should go to school, and the scheduling for special events such as birthdays and holidays

- possessions—who should occupy the family house or apartment (sometimes both spouses do, usually in separate bedrooms), who has control of any vehicles, and, if any property must be sold to produce cash, who should control the sale and how the proceeds should be handled

- protection orders—if there has been violence between the spouses, communications may be limited and restraining orders may be issued, (see "Dealing With Domestic Violence" in Chapter 10 for more detail on this), and

- enforcement—if an order made at trial has been violated, a motion may be filed to determine if the offending party should be punished (discussed in "Enforcing Court Orders" in Chapter 10). There is sometimes a need to enforce pretrial orders, too—such as an order for temporary support at trial. Many people work out some temporary answer to these problems voluntarily, but if that isn't happening, the court can only become involved if a pretrial motion is filed.

If you don't have a lawyer, a self-help center can normally help you prepare the motion, provide instructions on where to file it with the court, and tell you how to obtain a hearing date. (See "Legal Self-Help Centers" in Chapter 5.)

Pretrial motions will normally be heard by a judge who handles a group of similar cases at designated times each week. At the hearing, you will be expected to explain to the court why you need or oppose a pretrial order and, if relevant, to establish your own or your spouse's income. After the judge has ruled, the court may prepare an order reflecting the decision or may require you to prepare one for the judge to sign, making it legally enforceable.

Posttrial Motions

Posttrial motions are often required if there has been some change in circumstances since the last legal order took effect. Most of these motions request a modification of the trial judgment. For example, if one spouse was ordered to pay support but suddenly loses a job, he or she should get to court as soon as possible to ask for a reduction in the support payments. Or if a child visitation order is not working well because the children are unhappy about being left with baby-sitters for long periods, the court might be asked to change the order. These are modification motions.

Posttrial motions are prepared and filed in the same way as pretrial motions. Hearings on these motions and testimony before the judge will take place in the same way. The person seeking the relief must testify either orally or in a written declaration under penalty of perjury about why he or she is seeking the order.

In many cases, modifications cannot be made retroactive; the order made at a hearing is only effective from the date the motion was filed. For example, the court may not have the power to modify support payments that have accrued between the time a person lost a job and the date the motion to reduce the amount was filed.

Another variety of posttrial motion is an enforcement motion, usually known as an Order to Show Cause re Contempt, which requests that a person who is not complying with a court order be sentenced to jail. Most such motions relate to a failure to pay court-ordered child or spousal support. Others are related to violations of orders that one spouse stay away from the other, or for violating child visitation orders. (See "Enforcing Court Orders" in Chapter 10 for more details on these.)

> **SEE AN EXPERT**
> **You will need help in securing these orders.** Because of the severity of the punishment that may be ordered—five days in jail is no picnic—modification motions are somewhat complicated and are usually only successful when handled by an attorney. However, if you have no attorney, there are child support agencies in many states that will handle these motions for you if the facts are sufficiently serious.

Trials

There are two types of divorce trials: simple uncontested ones in which the spouses agree on all the terms of the divorce, and contested trials in which they disagree on some, or sometimes all, of the issues involved.

Uncontested divorces. Trials in uncontested divorces can usually be handled fairly easily by the spouses on their own without a lawyer's involvement. In some states, they can be handled by mail. Simplified procedures of this type are normally outlined in the local rules of your court—and some courts publish their rules on a website. Self-help agencies can also help make the best use of local procedures. (See Chapter 5 for more specifics on both of these resources.)

Where a personal appearance is necessary, the trial will usually take just a few minutes. In some cases, the judge will ask the necessary questions, which are described below—and all you have to do is say "Yes" several times—or perhaps "Yes, Your Honor."

Depending on your state, the person actually filing the divorce is referred to as the "petitioner," "plaintiff," or "complainant" and the other spouse is the "respondent or "defendant." In many cases, this is a legal fiction of sorts, since both spouses are anxious to get on with the process. But these are just legalistic labels to differentiate the parties.

You normally start by establishing your residence in the county and the length of your marriage: "I have lived in the state of _____ for (the time required in your state) and in the county of _____ for ___ months. We were married (date)."

You then must state some magic words establishing the state's acceptable reasons for the divorce. The required words vary from state to state, but they are easy to discover. You can find them out by visiting your courtroom when similar hearings are held sometime before your hearing date. You can also find them by going on the Internet to www. divorcesource.com, clicking on the heading "Grounds for Divorce," and then the name of your state. There you will see legal reasoning such as "irreconcilable differences which have caused the irremediable breakdown of the marriage."

In this example, the magic words you would need to tell the judge might be: "My spouse and I have irreconcilable differences which have caused the irremediable breakdown of the marriage." Or put a little less legalistically: "My spouse and I have had important differences that we cannot resolve and we believe that our marriage has permanently broken down."

Finally, hand the clerk any written settlement agreement that a lawyer or an Internet service has prepared for you or that you and your spouse prepared together. If only one of you is present in court, the other person should sign the agreement in front of a notary. Make a simple statement to the judge explaining the contents of the agreement, such as: "My spouse and I have agreed on the terms for our divorce as set forth in this agreement regarding support, custody of our children, and division of our property, and we request the court adopt it as part of our judgment of divorce." That should do it for an uncontested divorce.

And Then There's New York

New York is the only state that has not eliminated the old requirement that a person seeking a divorce must prove that his or her spouse is at fault for causing the break-up. New York requires that, unless the parties are willing to go through the year-long separation process described below, the moving party must allege cruel and inhuman treatment, imprisonment, adultery, or abandonment.

- Cruel and inhuman treatment is the grounds used most often. It is normally satisfied by testifying that your spouse called you bad names, started arguments, or was not affectionate. You should be able to identify two instances of this treatment over the past five years.
- Imprisonment must have lasted for a specific period of time, which you should check if you are unfortunate enough to qualify under this ground.
- The adultery ground requires sexual intercourse, either heterosexual or homosexual, with someone other than the spouse during the marriage and within the past five years. It requires the testimony from someone other than you and your spouse.
- Abandonment only works if it is "without provocation" and if you asked your spouse to come back home. It is proven either by establishing your spouse locked you out of your home or unjustifiably refused to have sexual relations for at least a year.

There is an alternate route for those who have a more sensitive taste and are willing to go through an only-in-NewYork jumble. It doesn't require you to say anything nasty about your spouse, but you must have settled all of the issues in your case in a written agreement filed with the court and have lived apart for a year. The state legislature has recently been urged to join the rest of the nation in providing an expeditious no-fault divorce, but so far it has resisted the entreaties of the lawyers, the judges, and the state's chief judge.

Another wacky part of the New York procedure is that is legally possible for you to have a jury trial on the sole issue of whether legal grounds for your divorce have been proven.

Contested divorces. By contrast, contested divorces—in which very little is agreed upon—are much trickier to navigate. In addition to complying with the complicated state laws controlling the issues in a divorce, you must also abide by the laws of evidence that control the types of testimony that are acceptable in court.

If your case is headed for a contested trial, the court will probably schedule a settlement conference before a mediator or judge with the hope of resolving some or all of the disputed issues. Some courts will automatically give you a date for a conference with a judge to check out settlement possibilities and to assign a trial date. Others require you to file a form requesting that the case be moved to trial. Check with your local clerk's office to see what procedure it follows.

Dates for contested trials are normally assigned at least a month in advance of the trial. The gap in time from when your case is filed at the clerk's office and when your trial begins will vary, depending on how busy the court is and how complicated your case appears to be. Some courts get a contested case to trial within 90 days of filing; others have such a backlog of cases waiting for trial that some cases are still not tried a year after they are filed.

CONSULT AN EXPERT

Contested divorces may require a lawyer's help. I have seen a few couples put on contested divorce trials without serious problems, but they have been rare. If you have come this far without a lawyer, consider getting some specialized information from a lawyer for this step as described in "Unbundled Legal Services" in Chapter 5.

Keeping the Evidence Up to Code

Evidence that is "admissible"—that is, that a judge will allow on the record and consider in making a final decision—is testimony or physical objects that meet the standards of the set of laws of your state, usually grouped in a statute called the Evidence Code, or something similar.

The laws controlling evidence law are not simple. Most law schools require students to take at least a year-long course in the subject before they can graduate. All of that learning comes into play when a lawyer jumps up in court and says something like: "Objection, Your Honor, that's irrelevant." Or: "No foundation." Or, the most common of all: "Hearsay"—which generally means that the person offering the evidence did not have personal knowledge of it.

After an objection is raised, the lawyer representing the other side normally expresses his or her disagreement with the objection. The judge then says either "sustained," meaning he or she agrees with the objection, or "overruled," which signals disagreement.

The Evidence Code can act to prevent a judge from hearing some evidence one of the parties thinks is important. Depending on what side of the case you are on, that result may seem fair . . . or unfair. But it is the law and must be followed.

For an excellent review of the basic rules of evidence, see *Represent Yourself in Court: How to Prepare & Try a Winning Case* (Nolo), by Paul Bergman and Sara Berman-Barrett.

Tips on Making a Courtroom Presentation

The first part of this chapter explained the situations in which you are required to be in court. This section contains some suggestions on how to conduct yourself once you get there—and includes a number of practical tips that may help make your courtroom presentation go more smoothly.

Keep in mind that every word that you, the judge, or anyone else who speaks in the case in court will be recorded by a court reporter or an electronic recording system. If you lose your cool and blurt out some inappropriate remarks, they will be preserved in the record for all to see for a very long time. And they might be reviewed by the judge when making a final decision.

> **TIP**
>
> **Some help from unexpected sources.** Because so many people process their divorces without lawyers, many courts have developed very helpful websites specially geared to people going through their divorce courts. So, in addition to the state websites described in Chapter 5, hunt around the Internet for sites that provide detailed family law information in your local court system. Begin by using a search engine and typing in the name of your county, and "divorce" and "court."

Write a Script

Before your court date, it is a good idea to write up a script designed to help you get what you want the judge to order at the end of the hearing.

The first step in doing this is to check the statute or rule that sets out the law on the subject. (See "Doing Your Own Legal Research" in Chapter 5 for details.) For example, if what you need is child support, look up your state's laws on how child support is determined. If you want your former spouse held in contempt of court for failing to pay child support, check out the details of the law on contempt.

The law will set out what elements the judge must consider in ruling on your issue. Jot them down and write out a script describing how you satisfy the requirements. Don't waste time with irrelevant issues that are not going to bear on the judge's decision.

For example, if you and your spouse are divorcing because of "irreconcilable differences" and you disagree about what to do with the marital home, a court exchange might go similar to the one below.

Clerk: Marriage of Johnson, Case Number 987453.

You: Ready, Your Honor. I am Harold Johnson, the petitioner in this case, and I request that I be sworn.

Judge: Is the respondent here?

Your spouse: Yes, Your Honor. I am Virginia Johnson.

Judge: Very well, swear the parties.

[Clerk swears you both to tell the truth.]

Judge: Go ahead, Mr. Johnson.

You: My wife and I were married June 11, 1997 and have resided in this county at all times since our marriage. We have developed irreconcilable differences, which have caused the irremediable breakdown of our marriage. We have reached agreement on all but one matter regarding the termination of our marriage. The agreed provisions are contained in the document I am handing to the clerk. [Hand the typed and signed agreement to the clerk.]

Judge: Ms. Johnson, is this your signature on the last page of this agreement? And do you agree to all of its terms?

Spouse: Yes, Your Honor.

Judge: I see you are waiving any right to receive alimony or spousal support from your husband, is that right?

Spouse: Yes, I have a good job and I don't need any support from him.

Judge: What is the matter on which you don't agree?

You: I want to sell our house now and split the proceeds. My wife wants to stay in the house for five years and then sell it.

Spouse: Judge, I have spent years turning our home, a former abandoned house, into a beautiful showpiece. I want to stay there for five years so that I can finish nursing school and get a good job.

Judge: Well, under the law, your husband is entitled to have his share of the property now. If you had a cosigner, you might be able to get an equity loan and buy your husband out. I'll give you 30 days to explore that. But in the meantime, I'll adopt your marital settlement agreement as the judgment of the court, restore you to the status of single people as of July 19 of this year and provide that if you are not able to reach an agreement on a buyout within 30 days, that the house be listed with ABC Real Estate Company and sold to the best offer within 60 days of listing. The net proceeds are to be split equally between you. You should prepare a judgment on the court's form, bring it to the clerk, and I will sign it. Court is in recess.

Another way to handle this situation is to hire a lawyer just to help you with the task of writing a script. (See "Unbundled Legal Services" in Chapter 5.)

> **WARNING**
>
> **Remain flexible.** While a script is an important part of your preparation for court, beware that you will need to remain flexible if the judge tells you to cover some other topic during your presentation. Just make sure you cover the judge's concerns succinctly and completely.

If you have relevant records that someone other than you prepared, you probably will not be able to have the judge consider them unless you have a witness who can personally authenticate them. This is because of the hearsay rule which, if is raised by the other party, prohibits you from introducing evidence that is not based on your firsthand knowledge. It also generally prohibits a witness from testifying about what another person said on a particular occasion.

For example, if you want to produce proof that your son doesn't get enough sleep when visiting with the other parent, you might bring in his teacher to testify that Mondays after visitation he sometimes falls asleep in class. Your testimony that your son told you he often stays up to midnight when he is at your spouse's house would violate the hearsay rule.

If you need the testimony of someone other than yourself to cover any of the legal issues, make arrangements to have that person in court on time.

Issues that might need the testimony from another witness may include:

- **financial matters**—if bank, pension, or real estate matters are important, you may need someone from a financial source to authenticate relevant records

- **support**—if your spouse has income he or she hasn't revealed, you may need a witness to prove that fact, and

- **custody**—teachers, baby-sitters, or other observers may be helpful in proving that your spouse is not the prize parent he or she claims to be.

If the necessary witness will not come to court voluntarily, obtain a subpoena from the court clerk's office and have it served on that witness. Laws differ on who can make the service. Check the Yellow Pages of your phone book for a local process server who will serve it for a fee; in most states, any adult who is not a party to your case can also do it. If in doubt, check with a lawyer's office or one of the legal self-help agencies discussed in Chapter 5.

> **TIP**
> **A road test can be well worth the mileage.** Once you know in what courtroom your proceedings will be held, it can be a good idea to try to make an exploratory trip to see how the judge and the staff there run things. This certainly isn't necessary, but if you are worried about your court appearance and have the time, a trip to see how the court operates can reduce stress. Some judges do different types of hearings on certain days of the week. So if you're going to investigate the courtroom this way, it would be a good idea to do it on the same day of the week you are scheduled to be in court.

Organize Your Papers

One of the most stressful moments in court can occur when a litigant can't find a paper that he or she wants to refer to when speaking. Paper goes flying, pulse rate rises—and the whole plan of the presentation can be lost.

To guard against this, put documents such as bank and financial records in one file, copies of the important papers that have been filed with the court in another, and papers such as old tax returns you want to use in still another. Clearly mark the files in the order you expect to need them in court.

The Clothing Issue

While it's true that appearance is important, way too many people spend way too much time worrying about what to wear to court.

Men: A coat and tie isn't necessary. Wearing jeans will not be fatal, but avoid them if possible. If all you have is work clothes or a uniform, wear a clean set of what you have.

Women: Heels and business attire aren't necessary; pants are fine. Fancy clothes and flashy jewelry are not a good idea.

While it's rare, some court rules actually address proper courtroom attire.

For example, Los Angeles Superior Court Rule 8.2 specifies that people appearing in the courtroom should not dress in an "inappropriate manner such as to be distracting to others of usual sensibilities." Most court administrators don't feel they need such a rule, but Los Angeles probably does.

Arrive on Time

There are few things that will cause greater stress on the day you must appear in court than arriving there late. Figure out in advance the route you will follow and how long it will take, factoring in commute hours if necessary—and know where you will park. Find out exactly where your courtroom is and on the day of your appearance, check the bulletin board in front of the courtroom for a posting—called the calendar— which should include the title of your case.

Sometimes the courtroom door will remain locked until just before the first scheduled hearing. When it opens, go up to the desk of the clerk, usually near the judge's bench, and tell him or her that you are checking in. In some courtrooms, the check-in process is handled by a person at a desk next to the rail that separates the audience from the rest of the courtroom. This may be a person in a law enforcement uniform called the bailiff—or, where budget cuts have been made, a civilian with a title such as "court attendant." After you check in, take a seat in the audience and wait for your case to be called.

Treat the Courtroom Staff Respectfully

Some inexperienced lawyers and people who are representing themselves in court don't realize that the staff and the judge who work together normally consider themselves as part of a team. As in many other workplaces, the staff commonly commemorate birthdays and other events by lunching or celebrating together.

When a lawyer or litigant gets snippy with one of the court personnel, the judge is sometimes informed when taking the bench by something as simple as a little mark on his or her copy of the calendar. This is not the way you want the judge introduced to your case.

When the judge comes on the bench, the bailiff normally gives either a short call, such as, "Remain seated and come to attention." Or a longer one, such as, "All rise. This court is now in session, the Honorable XYZ Presiding."

Some judges then ask you to join in saluting the flag.

The presiding judge may ask the clerk to swear in all people who will be testifying to tell the truth. If so, you and any witnesses you have with you should stand and repeat as required that you will tell the truth in your testimony. Then all you have to do is wait until your case is called. While waiting in the courtroom, don't read a newspaper, talk with people in the audience, or laugh loudly if some poor soul gets confused and flounders. It's okay, of course, to laugh if the judge attempts to make a joke.

If you have friends or witnesses with you, tell them it is very important that they not attempt to convey their reactions to testimony such as laughing or blurting out "That's a lie!" Nor should they do anything unusual such as storm angrily out of court when your opponent's lawyer is making a speech. And finally, they should not come up from the audience to pass you notes with their suggestions on strategy.

Observe Courtroom Etiquette

No matter how many legal shows you have seen on television, the courtroom is likely to feel like a foreign place, with rules of behavior all its own. Learning a bit of etiquette in advance will help ease your worries about making a gaffe.

When your case is called. Go forward and have a seat at the table in front of the judge called the counsel table. The space between counsel table and the judge's bench is called "the well," and you are expected to stay out of that area.

If you have not already been sworn, remain standing to be sworn by the clerk. If you have objections to taking an oath, tell the clerk that you would like to "affirm" instead of swear and when the words of the oath are stated, simply state "I affirm."

Addressing the judge. Most judges would rather be addressed as "Your Honor" rather than "Judge Smith." And when replying in disagreement with something the judge just said, avoid the phrase "With all due respect…" because most judges know that means the speaker doesn't feel very respectful.

Your job at the hearing is to convince the judge to give you the order you are seeking. It is not to get out the whole speech you wrote in your script and recited several times in the shower that morning. Most importantly, don't interrupt.

Arguing your case before a judge has nothing in common with arguing anything else in the world. There are arguments in life you win by just repeating over and over again why you are right and not listening to anything your opponent says. And there are arguments you can win by being louder and more forceful than the other side. These tactics never work when you are arguing your case before someone sitting in a black robe at a desk that is elevated above the floor you are standing on and who is called "Your Honor."

Judges appreciate persuasive arguments, but they want to be able to control your method of delivery and to be able to ask questions in the middle of your speech to be sure they understand your position.

Judges in divorce courts have probably heard the issue you are addressing several times in other cases. And they normally have some idea of what they consider the most important points on that issue. Some will remain stone-faced during your presentation, not giving you a clue about what they are thinking. And some will try to guide you to what they want to hear about. Some parties and lawyers understand the importance of these signals as to what the decision maker is thinking. Others don't understand its importance, ignore the judge's clue, and go right back to the script that they practiced.

For instance, suppose the issue before the court is how much alimony you should have to pay your spouse to maintain the standard of living you had while married. (See "The Alimony Amount" in Chapter 7 for details on this.) Subjects to be explored are: your capacity to pay, your spouse's ability to support himself or herself partially or totally, and the marital standard of living. Unknown to you, for example, the judge may have read through the file and already decided the answers to all questions but your spouse's ability to earn. The judge asks you to tell why you feel your spouse could earn more money by changing to another type of work. You'd never know what was bothering the stone-faced judge mentioned above. But if you ignore the comments of the more talkative judge, you are making a big mistake.

When you are speaking, direct your words to the judge, not to your spouse or anyone else in the courtroom. Arguing with your spouse in court will annoy the judge and damage the strength of your presentation. In referring to your spouse, use his or her last name, such as "Mr. Williams," or "Ms. Rafinelli," and speak as respectfully as possible, even if you are describing inappropriate conduct. You want to impress the judge with your reasonableness.

Don't talk over other speakers. In addition to being extra careful not to interrupt the judge, avoid interrupting anyone who is speaking during your hearing or trial. Not only is it rude, but it also makes it impossible for the court reporter to properly record what is taking place. If two people are talking at the same time, the reporter is likely to stop typing and say something about the problem you are causing. If the reporter's job is made more difficult by interruptions, the judge is likely to become irritated. This is not to your advantage.

Presenting a document to the judge. There is a little dance you must go through if you want the judge to look at and consider some document or other physical evidence in deciding some issue in your case. This might be last year's income tax return, the lease on your apartment or your car, or the "goodbye" letter your spouse left when moving out.

Step one: Hand the item to the clerk and say, "Please mark this item as an Exhibit." The clerk will take it, put a number or letter on it, such as "Exhibit 3," and hand it back to you.

Step two: Identify the item. For example, you might say: "Your Honor, Exhibit 3 is the income tax return my wife and I filed last year."

Step three: You say, "I move the item be admitted in evidence." If the judge says "Granted," or "Exhibit 3 is admitted in evidence," you've succeeded. If the judge says "Denied," you've lost. And if the judge doesn't immediately explain why, you might say something politely, such as: "I would appreciate it if Your Honor would indicate why you have denied my offer." Then perhaps you can repair the problem.

Don't Get Hung Up on Fairness

People who spend a lot of time worrying about whether or not something is "fair" tend to have serious problems while getting divorced. Deciding what's fair and what isn't can be a tough call on the playground, in business transactions, and in many other aspects of daily life. But nowhere is it more difficult than when breaking up a marriage.

If you are going to get divorced, keep this important fact straight: Most decisions in divorces are not based on what you, your soon-to-be ex-spouse, or a judge thinks would be fair. And in divorce court, arguing about whether something is fair is usually a waste of time. Divorce court decisions are made by applying laws and past case decisions to facts that are presented at your trial.

Despite these realities, human good sometimes triumphs over the odds. As quiet as it is kept, there is a sizable slice of the people going through divorce court who genuinely want to be fair to the spouse from whom they are getting divorced.

I have been in many settlement conferences when a husband says something like: "I want Betty to have enough money to be able to go to school part-time and I just don't think what she is asking for is enough. Let's make it $650 a month." Or a wife says: "You know, Frank, the children are going to want to see you on their birthday, so let's work out a plan that gives you some time with them on that day." When the other spouse smiles, looks across the table and says "Thanks," it's a good indication that fairness is happening.

Of course, everyone involved feels best when the judge's decision accomplishes something that seems fair. For example, if applying the law to a particular situation results in financial security for a parent who has struggled to hold the family together without moral or financial help from the other parent, the judge feels pleased making the necessary orders. And the family members will surely benefit from this legally imposed plan. But if the laws and court decisions of the state dictate a victory for a spendthrift philanderer, a judge has no choice but to follow the law and make a decision that most people would feel was unfair.

Intervening in the Name of Fairness

When I was sitting as a divorce judge, I would occasionally spot an agreement that looked terribly unfair and refuse to sign off until I had interviewed a party who was not represented by a lawyer.

One such case involved a retired member of the U.S. Navy who had been married to a Japanese woman for more than 20 years. Their major possession was his military pension and she had signed an agreement giving up all interest in it. Under the law controlling the case, a pension earned by one spouse during the marriage belonged equally to both.

A few days later when the husband appeared in court, I told him I wouldn't grant the divorce unless he brought his wife to court so that I could see if she understood she was giving up her legal interest worth several hundred thousand dollars. When they appeared together in court a few days later, I asked her if she understood that because the pension had all been earned while they were married, she was legally entitled to half of it.

In somewhat halting English, she said she understood and that she wanted him to have it all. She didn't seem clear on how she was going to support herself. Just then, the door in the back of the courtroom opened and a lawyer I recognized walked in with some papers to file. "Would you take Ms. Kramer here into my chambers and tell her about her rights under her husband's pension?" I asked the lawyer. She agreed and the women went behind closed doors for about 15 minutes while I handled another case.

When they reappeared, the wife had changed her mind. She wanted half of each pension payment. The husband saw there wasn't going to be a divorce if he didn't agree—and, with some grumbling, accepted the change, which was incorporated into their final divorce judgment.

When you are agreeing on issues at the kitchen table, meeting in mediation, or taking advantage of collaborative law, agreements you and your spouse make on your own based on fairness are just fine. (See Chapter 2 for more on these alternatives to divorce court.)

Judges will normally accept any settlement you and your spouse agree upon. But if you are not represented by a lawyer, a judge might feel that what you have agreed to is so far from what the law would provide that he or she will want to talk to you personally and be sure you understand your options. And the law in most states will also limit you from agreeing to provisions that would deprive your children of their legal rights.

But if you don't settle your case out of court, remember this: What a divorce court will do with your case will often not seem fair.

Why Divorce Courts Are Sometimes Unfair

Divorce courts are normally involved in deciding issues that the divorcing parties can't resolve themselves, such as:

- when allotting alimony or child support—how much money each spouse should be expected to earn
- when deciding custody matters—where the children should spend the majority of their time, and
- when divvying up a couple's property—what was in one of the spouse's savings account when they married.

There often is conflicting testimony by witnesses at a divorce trial on issues such as these, but once the judge decides whom to believe, he or she must apply the law as determined by the state legislature (statutory law) and by earlier decisions of higher state courts (precedent) when making a divorce judgment. In mathematical terms, the formula sounds simple: $F + L = J$ (facts plus law equals a judgment). In life, it's a difficult formula to apply.

Some people unfamiliar with the judicial system believe that trials are designed for judges to hear evidence and then decide what is fair. But there are two major reasons why they don't work that way: human subjectivity and the reality of the legal system.

Judges' Subjectivity

People looking at any human situation often disagree on what is fair. And, after all, judges are just people.

Contrary to the regimes in some other countries, American judges don't get any formal training on judging until after they have been appointed or elected. And even then, in many locales, the training is pretty spotty. Derek Bok, an author and former president of Harvard University, had this to say about how a person becomes a judge: "A judge is a member of the Bar who once knew a Governor."

Judges come from all political parties, many different religious or nonreligious beliefs, and very varied backgrounds. One judge I know grew up in a house with dirt floors and no plumbing. Some of them grew up in mansions and attended exclusive private schools.

Individual experience and beliefs should not control the outcome of a case. Making an individual judge's concept of fairness the basis for a ruling would be just plain unfair. However, personal history and exposure are bound to affect what every judge thinks is fair in situations that come into his or her courtroom.

I am a great admirer of a statement that a British judge, Lord Denning, made in 1981: "My root belief is that the proper role of a judge is to do justice between the parties before him. If there is any rule of law which impairs the doing of justice, then it is the province of the judge to do all he legitimately can to avoid that rule—or even to change it—so as to do justice in the instant case before him."

I have quoted this in several cases in which I felt I was dealing with an unfair law. But in truth, a trial judge's attempt to avoid or change a law is not often successful. The bottom line is the same as the line at the top of this chapter: Don't get hung up on fairness.

Courts don't—and you shouldn't either.

Defining Fairness

Legal scholars have attempted to define justice and fairness for hundreds of years. Benjamin N. Cardozo, once one of America's most revered justices of the U.S. Supreme Court, might have come closest in his famous lectures on "The Nature of the Judicial Process" in 1921.

Discussing what a judge should do when faced with deciding an issue that no court has ruled on, he said: "There is nothing to do except to have some impartial arbiter declare what fair and reasonable men, mindful of the habits of life of the community, and of the standards of justice and fair dealing prevalent among them, ought in such circumstances to do, with no rules except those of custom and conscience to regulate their conduct."

Addressing the same subject, Justice Felix Frankfurter, Cardozo's successor on the Supreme Court, said: "The highest exercise of judicial duty is to subordinate one's personal pulls and one's private views to the law of which we are all guardians—those impersonal convictions that make a society a civilized community and not the victims of personal rule."

Structure of the Legal System

The American justice system requires that exactly the same laws and principles must be applied to every case that comes through the courts.

The problem with this that most of the laws that control in divorce cases are made in state legislatures, where those who actually make the laws rarely see the complicated human tangles that appear in divorce courts. In too many instances, the laws just don't fit into the reality of what is happening in courts—or in human lives.

When the Law Is an Ass

The most unfair result in any case I have been part of involved Terri and Elliott. The couple had moved to Alaska at Elliott's insistence, where they homesteaded and built a cabin 12 miles from the nearest town. Elliott took a job 200 miles away, while Terri, five months pregnant, remained at the cabin. She testified that during the winter months, the cabin was so cold that standing water inside would freeze. They had no plumbing and carried water in five-gallon containers from a stream nearby. Terri split the wood, broke up coal with a sledge hammer, and used a sled or wheelbarrow to bring in laundry and food. After seven years, the couple returned to the San Francisco area so that Elliott could attend law school. He eventually became a lawyer and opened his own practice.

For 21 years, the parties held themselves out as husband and wife to the Internal Revenue Service and their banks and insurance companies. They bought and sold real estate as husband and wife. But they never actually got married. Meanwhile, Terri had several surgeries for a herniated disk and began wearing a back brace. She had to hire help to run the household where she lived with the couple's three children after they separated.

Terri filed for something akin to a divorce, and because it was clear it might take several years for the case to come to trial, she requested temporary support pending trial. I granted her request. But a higher court reversed my decision and held that the only way she could get temporary support would be if the legislature passed a new law allowing an unmarried partner to get it. Disagreeing with the ruling of the other justices, Justice Marc Poche wrote: "The result reached by the majority may be, in the eyes of some, good law; it is lousy justice."

Was the decision fair? Of course not. But it has not been overruled or criticized by other courts since it was issued well over a decade ago. So it was—and still remains—the controlling law.

But if we didn't have laws that all judges must apply in deciding each and every case, the judicial system would be so unpredictable that our society would be in a constant state of confusion. In fact, the positive side of this one-size-fits-all approach is that with well-known laws and precedents available, lawyers are usually able to predict what would happen at a trial and advise their clients on a reasonable settlement. And once a judge zeros in on the facts of a particular case and decides what testimony to believe, he or she can usually find and apply the controlling law fairly easily. That wouldn't be possible if judges' decisions rested entirely on subjective views of fairness. ●

Know How and Where to Get Legal Help

n truth, it's difficult to go through the process of getting divorced without at least some type of legal assistance. And unless you are a very committed do-it-yourselfer, there is no reason you should brave it completely alone.

There are several possible sources to which you can turn to get helpful advice—ranging from paying a lawyer to handle everything, to representing yourself with the assistance of a self-help book. There also are nonlawyer paralegals in many communities who will help with the legal paperwork on an uncomplicated divorce for a cost similar to what an experienced divorce lawyer charges for an hour of time. Many state courts have websites that provide excellent advice on how to do your divorce without a lawyer. And there are free self-help law centers available in quite a few communities. This chapter discusses all of these options—and explains when and how to proceed with the one that's most sensible for you.

Whether you choose to hire legal help and what type of help you choose should depend on:

- how complicated your case is
- how much money you want or are able to spend for assistance
- whether you have the time and patience to fight your way alone through the forms, bureaucracy, and legalese involved
- whether there is a decent chance you and your spouse can reach agreements on the issues that are involved in your divorce
- whether you believe that having your case handled by a lawyer could help to isolate your children from the contentious moments that might otherwise occur if you and your spouse deal directly with one other, and
- whether you are the type of person who would rather control every aspect of your case instead of operating through a lawyer as intermediary.

> ### The Thorny Matter of Cost
>
> While you can pay several hundreds of dollars an hour to get the services of an experienced divorce lawyer, there are many very good ones across the country who charge between $100 and $200 an hour for their services. And as explained later in this chapter, there are ways you can use a lawyer for just a portion of your divorce and do the simpler parts by yourself. (See "Unbundled Legal Services," below.)
>
> If you want the assistance of a lawyer, but don't have the money that would be required to hire one, check out the website at www.lawhelp.org. It contains information about agencies that provide legal help to people who have low or moderate incomes, county by county across the nation.

Deciding Whether to Go It Alone

No matter how straightforward your case is, it will likely move faster and easier if you have a competent lawyer to oversee it from beginning to end. But it often makes sense to proceed without one. Some of the situations that are particularly suitable for handling without a lawyer's help are those in which:

- the marriage has lasted no more than two or three years and there are no children and few possessions and debts to be divided

- the marriage lasted longer than three years, but you and your spouse have reached a written agreement on what all the terms of the divorce should be—called an "uncontested divorce" (see "A Glossary of Divorce Jargon" in Chapter 1 for a detailed definition), and

- your spouse is likely to ignore and fail to file an answer to the divorce papers you serve on him or her, giving you the right to proceed uncontested—in what is called a "default divorce" (see "A Glossary of Divorce Jargon" in Chapter 1 for a detailed definition).

Situations in which it would be particularly difficult to proceed without a lawyer include those in which it seems unlikely that the spouses will be able to agree about how to divide assets such as substantial retirement rights earned during the marriage, stock options, or a house or business that will have to be liquidated. Cases in which the couple disagrees about where the children will live or the true earnings each spouse has are also difficult to handle without a lawyer's assistance.

Legal Help Other Than Lawyers

This section reviews the many alternatives to hiring a lawyer to handle your divorce. Which alternative you may choose to use largely depends on what resources are available where you live—and that varies greatly from community to community.

Court Websites

While courts and the legal profession have generally been slow to embrace technological advances, most state courts now have official Internet sites that give information to help people navigate through their divorce procedures. If you live in a state with a good website, this is by far the best place for you to start putting your case together.

The following states provide the most comprehensive sites—generally including the forms you will need, local resources for more help, and procedural rules: Alaska, Arizona, California, Colorado, Connecticut, Florida, Georgia, Hawaii, Indiana, Maryland, Minnesota, Montana, Nevada, New Mexico, New York, Oregon, Pennsylvania, Utah, Washington, and Wisconsin. Less helpful, but still worthwhile are sites for Arkansas, District of Columbia, Idaho, Illinois, Iowa, Idaho, Nebraska, New Jersey, Michigan, and North Carolina. The remaining states were slower to get on the Internet bandwagon, and have sketchy sites—or no sites at all. But the trend is positive, and it is worth checking to see what your state offers, no matter where you live.

You can find the addresses for all state court sites on the website of the National Center for State Courts, an organization that, among other things, gathers information on self-help resources in family law. There is a link to its compendium of state self-help resources at: www.ncsconline. org/wcds/edu/prosestatesum.htm.

There are four topics linked on the page:

- The first one provides basic information for each state.

- The second concerns unbundled legal services, discussed later in this chapter.

- The third, Self-help/Information Resources and Centers, provides some information that basically supplements the first topic in some states—and gives information about what legal self-help services are available locally.

- The fourth link in most states will provide the current divorce court forms. Many states make the use of their forms mandatory. Some states hide the forms under a somewhat mysterious heading that will require a little sleuthing on your part to find, but it is worth your time. Beware that some websites charge for the forms they offer. For example, there is a commercial Internet site that charges almost $50 for the same material. But at the National Center for State Courts site mentioned here, you can be confident the forms are current and will be accepted at the court; outdated forms and information are a common drawback to many of the self-help resources available.

While checking these resources, you might find that the entries for some states only include information on a court in one large county. If you do not live in that county, follow the general directions provided, anyway; the provisions will be very similar to those for your county.

WARNING

Take cautions with a grain of salt. A few of the court websites appear to be written by lawyers or representatives from state bar associations and warn that it's essential to consult a lawyer. For example, the site for Lancaster County, Pennsylvania, cautions that if you proceed without a lawyer, "it will take a lot of time and cause you difficulty, confusion, and frustration." And it adds: "Speaking with an attorney is absolutely recommended if you wish to bring up issues besides legally ending your marriage." It's a pity this extravagant statement, which in my opinion is not true, was included. However, the site contains some other redeeming information.

The Arrival and Growth of Self-Help Law

Statistics gathered by the American Bar Association indicate that in 1990, 52% of divorcing families obtained a divorce without either side having an attorney. In 88% of divorce cases, one party had an attorney, but the other did not. There has been no comprehensive nationwide study made since 1990. However, available figures from several states indicate the numbers of those who opt to represent themselves have risen since then—and perhaps are now leveling off.

Some have charged that the self-help divorce movement is limited to people with low incomes and little education. But statistics suggest the contrary. A study done for the American Bar Association in Phoenix showed that 90% of unrepresented litigants had at least a high school education with an average of one to three years of college. More than half had an annual income of $30,000 or less, but quite a few made more than $50,000 a year.

These litigants said they had three major reasons for representing themselves:

- The matter was relatively simple and they could handle it themselves—45%.
- They could not afford a lawyer—31%.
- They did not want to pay a lawyer even though they could afford one—22%.

Self-represented litigants had the same level of positive reaction to their court experiences as those with counsel: 64% as compared to 63%. And 70% said they would represent themselves again so long as the other side didn't have a lawyer, in which case only 36% would represent themselves.

Legal Self-Help Centers

There are local centers in many cities from which you can obtain assistance as you process your divorce. Services will vary depending on the center you use, but at the very least, you should be able to obtain the legal forms needed to start your divorce and some instructions on what to put in any confusing blanks and boxes on the form. You should also be able to get help in using the state's formula for setting child support (see "Determining Child Support" in Chapter 8 for details on this) and directions for how to proceed with your case through the local courts.

Many programs, such as the Maricopa County Self Service Center described below, are available to anyone seeking information. Other programs have income limits for their clients or serve only people who have children.

Some programs, such as the Friend of the Court offices in Michigan and the Family Law Facilitator offices in California, are part of court systems and provide help with specific types of issues in divorces, such as obtaining child and spousal support. The California Facilitator service, for example, is provided without charge to anyone requesting help on the subjects of child support, alimony, and parentage. The facilitators involved are all lawyers; San Diego County has 17 facilitators. Los Angeles County contributes funding of more than $1 million a year to self-help centers and, operating through a grant from the federal AmeriCorps program, has established a program called JusticeCorps, in which 100 college students will be trained to provide legal workshops and assistance in filling out court forms.

In addition to the websites mentioned above, a good place to find out what self-help centers are available in your area is at the nearest law library. Law libraries are attached to law schools or located in most county seats and in all large cities, and the librarians there should be able to direct you to local self-help programs.

If you can't find a helpful law librarian, representatives at your city or county bar association may also know about available self-help programs. And in smaller communities, the clerk in the superior or domestic relations court may be helpful. At the very least, the clerk may be able to provide you with the forms you will be required to fill out to get your case started.

The Cream of the Self-Help Center Crop

The self-help center in Maricopa County, Arizona, is one of the most impressive in the country. Built with the help of a large grant from the Ford Foundation, the center is in a spacious modern building with facilities to serve anyone seeking direction in a divorce. The center is well-used by locals and frequently visited by those planning new centers from all over the nation. Video instruction and a large library are available. And there are packets of forms for every type of case, including detailed information on how to fill out and file them. The center is also staffed with trained volunteers to answer questions and a directory of local attorneys and qualified mediators willing to help people with limited incomes.

The thing that impressed me most about the center was that the people who came there for assistance were treated with respect and care. I have heard about a few self-help centers at which the people behind the counter treat their customers with disdain, suggesting that they are somehow doing something wrong in attempting to navigate their divorces without a lawyer. This is definitely not true in Maricopa County.

Independent Paralegals

SKIP AHEAD

Check availability. Before you read this section describing independent paralegal services, check to see whether such services are available in your community. Independent paralegals are listed in the Yellow Pages under headings such as Divorce Assistants, Paralegals, Legal Document Assistants, and Legal Clinics. If you find a listing under such a title and you would like to avoid hiring a lawyer, read on. Otherwise, skip to the next section on "Internet Document Preparation Services" to see whether this option might offer the help you need, instead.

First, a bit of history. It used to be that the only paralegals anyone saw were those who worked in law offices as assistants to lawyers. They interviewed walk-in clients to see if they had a case the firm could handle, did research, and gathered reports and documents for cases.

In the early 1980s, it became apparent to some of these employees that they could have their own businesses filling out the forms for people who had legal problems—and so they struck out on their own as "independent paralegals." Most charged less than half of what a starting lawyer charged for services and many of them prospered. Lawyers, of course, became upset with this development and urged district attorneys in some communities to prosecute a number of independent paralegals for practicing law illegally.

But in time, paralegals have become recognized as a possible source of helpful assistance for people who can't or don't want to hire lawyers. In 1998, California became the first state to officially recognize paralegals as "legal document assistants," who must meet certain education requirements, be bonded, and register with the county clerk in any county in which they practice.

In 2003, Arizona adopted a court rule regarding "legal document preparers," who must meet educational requirements and pass a test.

Florida created a system of simplified court forms and provided that it was not a violation of the law for nonlawyers to assist people in filling in the forms and providing some limited instruction.

Paralegals now operate independently in many other states, particularly Minnesota, Nevada, Oregon, Texas, and Washington. "We The People," a franchise paralegal organization, operates in 31 states.

Paralegals are prohibited by law from giving legal advice. They can't go to court with you or draft a Marital Settlement Agreement from scratch. They can, however, prepare the forms for your divorce, tell you where and when to file them, and describe how to serve the papers on your spouse. If your state has its own forms for requesting or modifying child support or alimony, paralegals can fill them out for you.

Using paralegals for these sorts of tasks in an uncomplicated case can make things move quickly and a lot less expensively than using a lawyer. But in a complex or hotly contested case, paralegals can offer only very limited help. And because paralegals can't give you legal advice, they may not be able to answer some of the questions you have. However, they can refer you to books and other targeted resources that may be helpful.

One potential problem with independent paralegals is that other than in Arizona and California, there is no system to qualify or regulate them—and some dishonest people have gone into the business and botched cases in the guise of providing help.

Here are some areas to check out if you are searching for a qualified paralegal to hire.

Ask about training and education. Many community colleges and university extension programs offer rigorous programs in the field and a person who has completed such a program should have written evidence to prove it.

Check with your local better business bureau. Find out whether there have been any complaints about a particular individual's services before you hire him or her.

Ask a local attorney for a reference. Some family law lawyers have reciprocal agreements in which recommendations are made back and forth with a reliable paralegal.

Find out how long the paralegal has been in business. Ask the paralegal how much experience he or she has—but also inquire about how long he or she has been in business at that particular location. Those who have less than desirable pedigrees seem to float in and out of business with different offices and phone numbers.

Ask for a written agreement. Before you hire any individual independent paralegal, ask to see a written agreement setting out exactly what services will be performed—and what the charges will be for each of them.

A Paralegal Who Felt the Long Arm of the Law

Several years before my retirement, I began to notice that some of the people representing themselves in court were submitting forms and notices of motions that had been typed in a professional manner, but just didn't make sense. Each of them told me their papers had been prepared by a particular local paralegal. I looked in the Yellow Pages and found a quarter-page advertisement in the fellow's name, with a photograph of a smiling group of people of various races holding hands.

Shortly thereafter, a man came to see me about having paid the same paralegal $1,000 for services that were never provided. His calls to the paralegal's office went unanswered. I referred the miffed customer to the Consumer Affairs Bureau of the district attorney's office.

I later got a subpoena to appear at a criminal trial for the owner of the paralegal office. The paralegal, now the defendant in the case, had fired his lawyer and was representing himself, rather poorly. At his jury trial, the district attorney examined me quickly and turned me over to the defendant for cross-examination. Tellingly, the paralegal couldn't seem to get out a question that made sense and several of the jurors squirmed in their seats as he blundered again and again. He was convicted of three misdemeanors and sentenced to more than a year in the county jail.

Several months later, a deputy sheriff at the county jail where the defendant was imprisoned told me of another problem the fellow had experienced. The deputy said the prisoner was giving legal advice to other prisoners on how to handle their court appearances. Then one day the deputy noticed the former paralegal limping through the dining hall with major bandages over the side of his head. It turned out he had given some bad legal advice to a man being tried on some serious felonies and that the recipient of the advice had come back from court and expressed his unhappiness—with his fists.

Internet Document Preparation Services

Several Internet websites call themselves online divorce services and advertise that they can give you all the help you need to get divorced; you simply need to fill out a questionnaire on your computer and pay their fees in addition to a court filing fee. Based on your answers, the services promise to prepare all of the necessary documents, send them to you and your spouse for signatures—and then file them by fax with your local court. Most such services only cover uncontested cases—those in which both of the parties agree on every issue in the divorce.

As mentioned above, there are also sites on the Internet that offer to send you all the blank forms you will need to do a divorce by yourself—although some of them don't require you to specify what state you want to file in, so their forms are not likely state-specific. Beware that generic forms are useless and destined to cause the person who uses them great frustration when they are later rejected by the court.

Self-Help Books

Books that purport to help you do your whole divorce by yourself are available from several sources. Some attempt to guide you through the procedure of every state in one book, others deal with only a single state.

While the information that a nationwide book provides on the law of your state can be helpful, court procedures vary so much, even within a state, that such a book doesn't do the job it promises. The national books are too often filled with disclaimers about state law differences to offer any true and specific guidance. So if you are considering representing yourself, you will usually get the best help from a book that focuses on the law in your state. To see what is available in your state, go to a site such as Amazon.com and type in "Divorce and (your state)." You will get a long list of books that may or may not be helpful. Or do your search the old-fashioned way: by browsing the shelves of a local library or bookstore.

Importantly, look for a book that is no more than a year or two old. Check for books that include the court forms necessary to get divorced—and have good guidance on what forms you need and how to fill them out.

Taking a Test Drive—Or Two

My only experience with Internet divorce preparation programs occurred several years ago when a reporter for *People* magazine asked me to go online, use some hypothetical facts, and then evaluate a particular online divorce service. After she assured me that her employer would pay the filing fee, which amounted to several hundred dollars, I logged on and spent more than an hour wandering through hundreds of questions that attempted to cover all the issues that could ever arise in the most complicated divorce ever imagined.

The program rejected some of the perfectly straight answers I typed in and left me so frustrated that I finally just gave up. It seemed that the mastermind behind the program knew enough to cover the issues that would come up in a normal divorce, but had gotten so tangled in the relationships among all of the questions that the initial questionnaire just wasn't helpful.

A really responsible horse of a different color is available in California at www.divorcehelp.com, where attorneys will work with spouses by telephone or in person to do an entire uncontested divorce. The service, operated by one of Nolo's original founders, Ed Sherman, charges a set fee of $1,995 to prepare all of the documents including a marital settlement agreement, mediate disputes, and consult about any related concerns you have. The Frequently Asked Questions section of the website points out some of the possible dangers of hiring an attorney to start your divorce.

If more than one book has court forms, choose the one with the most recent publication date, because these forms are typically revised frequently. Then, before you use the forms, go to your state self-help website and compare any forms available there with the ones in your book. Do not use any that have been superseded. A common consumer complaint is that the forms included in a bound book were outdated—and so rejected by a local court.

A Look Between Two Covers

One of the national divorce books recommends that you go to your local court and ask to review the file of another couple that recently got divorced. You are directed to buy copies of the documents in the file and use them for a guide in preparing your forms. If the clerk requires that you have the names of the parties when you ask for the files, the book suggests you consult your local newspaper for the names of people who have been divorced recently and to use those names to request a file.

This is just plain silly, for a number of reasons. First, the busy clerks in most courts are very unlikely to volunteer to hunt through the file room to find what you want. They generally provide files by case numbers to people who know the number of the case they want to review.

Second, cases are so different that, even if the clerk would honor your request, you would have to go through stacks of files before you found one that had facts that were even remotely close to your situation.

Finally, it would be tough for you to determine what papers might be relevant to your own case. Most forms are so complicated that it would take you hours to copy them in longhand. If the clerk's office has facilities to make copies, the charge per page is probably quite high. You will obviously not be allowed to take original documents out of the office.

To be helpful, a self-help book should contain a fair amount of explanation of the specifics of your state law. If you can find such a book for your state and if it appears to be written by someone with good credentials, give it a try.

WARNING

Checking a book for outdated information. Your ability to check out the current validity of a form in a book may depend on locale. As a test, I recently tried this process of updating on the Internet for three books for an Illinois divorce. The most recent book was only months old, but I could find no state site that provided forms for comparison with those in the book. Two of the sites had closed down and the other one, the Self Help Center at the Southern Illinois University School of Law, offered to mail a package of forms, but stated one should allow two weeks for the forms to arrive. It also indicated they could not be used in Cook County. I ordered the forms, and they arrived promptly with an extremely helpful set of directions on how to use them. I tried the same procedure in Indiana. That state's website makes all of the forms available for download online. If you can't check the forms you find online, it is a good idea to visit your local court and pick up a packet of forms there.

Hiring a Lawyer

If you decide to hire a lawyer to help with your divorce, it is important to choose one who is a good fit for you and your situation.

There are several reasons why you might not fit well with a particular lawyer. Some potential clients are clear from the start that they want a lawyer who is of the same gender they are. Others reject a lawyer who seems too aggressive, opting instead for a more soothing or parental type. For some, aggressiveness is a prized trait. Price can also be a consideration; when there are lawyers available for $150 an hour, many people steer clear of those charging twice that much.

TIP

Getting a court-ordered loan. If you don't have the money to hire a lawyer and your spouse has far greater financial resources than you do, a judge may order your spouse to advance funds to enable you to hire an attorney. Knowing this, some lawyers will charge only a minimal retainer to file the first appearance paper in your case—normally known as a complaint or petition—and then prepare a motion requesting you be advanced fees by your spouse to compensate your lawyer. The supporting papers will tell the judge that without such an order, you won't be able to afford legal representation. If the judge orders fees, the lawyer will continue to represent you. However, the lawyer is likely to bow out without such an order—and no clear promise of payment.

The Case of the Bumbling Barrister

There are few things more uncomfortable than realizing in the middle of a trial that your lawyer is blowing your case because he or she doesn't know the law or how to operate effectively in court.

I witnessed that very thing a few years ago in a case that involved a lawyer's attempt to prove that a husband had lied under oath about when he first learned that he was the father of a child with whom he had been acquainted for some time. He testified early in the trial that he had only learned the fact recently.

Unbeknownst to the husband, however, the wife's lawyer had obtained a copy of an old tax return that the husband had filed, listing the child as his daughter. Obviously, the return was something most would consider "a smoking gun"—and essential to get into evidence. But for this lawyer, that was easier said than done.

Lawyer: I think the husband's testimony is refuted by his tax returns, where he clearly listed her as a dependent and specifically as a daughter.

Judge [me]: Those documents are not in front of me.

Lawyer: They are in evidence.

Me: You have never offered them in evidence.

Lawyer: Well, I thought I did. Can I offer them now?

Me: I hate to go into the rudiments of trial practice which I teach at [a local law school], but there are three steps for getting a document into evidence. First you have it marked by the clerk with a number. That's step number one. Step number two: Through a witness or other means, you have it verified. And then, number three, you say "Your Honor, I move this item be admitted in evidence."

Lawyer: Okay.

Me: And only then can the judge look at it.

Lawyer: [law school where I taught] is my alma mater. And I now wish I'd taken your class.

Types of Lawyers

Finding a lawyer who is a good fit can be challenging. It's not that there aren't fine, sensitive, and ethical divorce lawyers nearby who would be happy to represent you; there are lawyers that meet that description almost everywhere. But there are also many who aren't strong in their knowledge of the law, don't care much about your personal needs, or charge too much for what they do. And there are more than a few who are deficient in all those respects.

So clearly, one key task is to get a short list of high quality local divorce lawyers who charge within your price range. (See "Steps in Finding a Lawyer," below.) And another is to be attuned to what may be less obvious: the type or combination of types of divorce lawyer for which you search.

Here are some types that I have identified over the years.

The Bomber. The Bomber (discussed in "Combative Counsel Is Involved" in Chapter 2) may regale you with stories about how he or she demolished the other side in a recent trial—as in: "I had the husband so confused on the stand that the judge finally had to jump in and call a recess." A Bomber will shun mediation and collaborative law. In this lawyer's view, the only time to talk about settlement is after the other side has been decimated and is pleading for mercy.

The Gender Specialist. There are some lawyers who advertise that they only represent clients of one gender. Their pitch is that the court assigned to hear your case discriminates against whichever gender they specialize in and that you need a lawyer who knows how to deal with that. They may go on and on about how "wives always try to turn the kids against their husbands" or "husbands always have some money squirreled away somewhere." In reality, the best lawyers usually represent as many men as they do women. Gender Specialists have a fairly harmless gimmick, but one that doesn't usually ring true—and if practiced too zealously, may actually alienate a judge.

The Lawyer Who Suffered From Ego Inflation

A recent article in a legal newspaper quoted a Los Angeles lawyer as saying that when he goes into a divorce trial, he has a specific plan for exactly how he is going to present the evidence and argument. He complained, however, that too many judges interrupt him in mid-presentations, asking questions and suggesting solutions. Sometimes, he said, they lecture him or the parties about concerns they have about how the well-being of the children is not being appropriately considered.

What the lawyer didn't seem to understand is the fact that in a divorce trial, the ultimate decision is in the judge's hands alone. If the judge believes the attorney is going on with irrelevancies and not dealing with important issues, it is the judge's duty to inquire and to ask for evidence on issues he or she feels are crucial.

A lawyer's game plan may be beautifully drawn, but it is useless if it doesn't cover the issues that concern the judge.

The Settler. Most family lawyers know that more than 90% of the cases they handle settle before trial. But some lawyers don't want to tell a prospective client this at the start because they think the client may fear the lawyer will sell them out cheaply to avoid a trial. The Settler will tell the client that he or she will fight to get all of the important financial facts on the table in the early stages of the case, but once that is done, those involved can almost always work out a good settlement that will avoid a trial.

The High-Priced Star. There are a few lawyers in most communities who have reputations as the top divorce lawyers in the area. They usually have beautiful offices, large staffs of assistants, and expensive cars—some with chauffeurs. Most charge between $300 and $500 an hour for their services, and they rarely finish a case for less than $20,000. In my experience, most of these lawyers have earned reputations for their skills, but in the final analysis are not significantly more skilled than many other good lawyers who are much less expensive.

The General Practice Lawyer. This lawyer doesn't specialize in family law, but may well be competent to handle uncomplicated family law matters. Some general practitioners will assure you that a specialist isn't necessary. However, if you have decided to hire a lawyer, it is usually preferable to find one who specializes in family law. Appellate courts frequently make changes in the fine points of family law and a generalist can't be expected to stay current on these matters. If you live in a small community where there is no lawyer who specializes in family law, consider checking out a specialist in a larger neighboring area to take your case.

Unbundled Legal Services

A growing number of lawyers will agree to handle just a part of your divorce case and leave the rest of it for you to do on your own. This practice is called "unbundling," referring to the fact that there are several tasks in a case which might be characterized as a bundle of sticks. Lawyers are normally hired to handle the entire bundle. The lawyer who agrees to provide unbundled services will allow you to take the bundle apart and choose who will handle each of the sticks. For example, you might agree that you would handle any court appearances by yourself— or with a little coaching from the lawyer—and that he or she would draft court documents and any settlement agreement that is reached.

For many years, attorneys shied away from such a practice because they were worried clients would give them only partial information, use their advice, and then sue them for malpractice if things didn't work out as expected. But the idea of "unbundled legal services" or "limited representation" is now growing—based on the idea that it makes sense for a lawyer to allow a client to order just the amount of legal help that is needed in a particular case.

There are several reasons you may want to consider this approach. Maybe you have a basic distrust of lawyers, so want to use as little of their services as possible. Or possibly you want to maintain tight control over important issues in your case. Or perhaps you'd like to save some money by doing some of the legal work yourself.

What It Means to Be a Family Law Specialist

Some states—including Connecticut, Maryland, Oklahoma, Utah, and West Virginia—don't allow lawyers to advertise a specialty in family law or any other specialty. Other states provide only that lawyers may advertise that they "choose" to practice in a specific field such as family law. This does not necessarily mean that such lawyers have had any special education or experience in the field.

The majority of states provide that only an attorney who has met the requirements set out below may advertise as a "certified specialist in family law." But the title often comes with a caveat. New York, for example, requires that when making such an advertisement, lawyers must add: "Certification does not necessarily indicate greater competence than other attorneys experienced in this field of law." It is easy to imagine the argument that went on in the New York bar before these words were inserted in their rule: Those who didn't want to go through the demanding requirements for certification didn't want to lose clients to those who became certified.

According to the American Bar Association, the nation's largest association of lawyers, to be certified as a specialist under most certification programs, lawyers must:

- provide evidence of substantial involvement in the specialty area and appropriate references from lawyers and judges
- take a written examination in the substantive and procedural law in the specialty area
- show that they have completed at least 36 hours of continuing legal education courses in the specialty area in the three-year period before applying for certification
- be admitted to practice and a member in good standing in at least one state
- be recertified at least every five years and be subject to revocation of certification if they fail to continue to meet the program's requirement.

To check your state in more detail, go to the American Bar Association's website at www.abanet.org/legalservices/specialization/state.html and click your state.

Be aware that there are some very good divorce lawyers who choose not to go through the rigorous certification process and others who just haven't yet tried the requisite number of cases. And in many cases the cost of hiring a specialist may be more than you want to pay.

TIP

Check out specific state rules. Some states have rules on how lawyers and clients must conduct an unbundled relationship. Specific state rules are gathered on the National Center for State Courts website at www.ncsconline.org/wc/publications/statelinks/proseunbunstatelinks.htm.

In an unbundled relationship, an attorney may agree to perform selected services provided that you sign an agreement specifying that he or she does not represent you or have full responsibility for handling your case. This agreement is something that should be very important to you both because it radically changes the traditional attorney/client relationship. And some local rules specifically require attorneys to file a document with the court explaining the scope of the limited services they will perform for their clients.

Those limited services may include:

- explaining your legal rights and responsibilities about specific issues
- advising about how to obtain information from banks, credit card companies, and other financial sources on accounts you or your spouse hold
- helping you to develop a negotiation strategy
- teaching you how to present evidence in court
- filling out forms
- writing letters or court documents
- accompanying you to a mediation session, and
- reviewing mediated or negotiated agreements.

There is no central directory of lawyers who offer unbundled services, but if you phone a lawyer's office and ask the receptionist whether unbundled services are offered there, you probably will get a quick answer. If the person answering the phone doesn't know what unbundling means, that is probably a strong indication that the lawyer working there doesn't offer such services.

Steps in Finding a Lawyer

In the past, many people relied upon a trusted barber, beautician, bartender, or someone else in the community who knew the local scuttlebutt for recommendations about the best lawyer to hire. But divorce law was much simpler a generation or two ago, and back then, almost any lawyer could do a creditable job on a garden variety case. Unfortunately, family law has gotten much more complicated in the last few decades—especially when a case involves a sizable amount of money and property. Barbers, beauticians, bartenders, and other community sages are probably as likely to recommend a showy self-promoter, who is more than unlikely a bad fit for your needs.

In truth, there is no surefire way to find the perfect lawyer to hire, but here are some suggestions and logical steps to take.

Step One: Ask for Personal Recommendations

Ask knowledgeable people in your community for the names of lawyers you might hire for help with your divorce. For leads, it is generally best to rely on somebody you know fairly well. Ideally, the person you consult will be someone who has been around a bit and will know to steer you away from one who doesn't have the qualities you are seeking. A marriage counselor, an accountant, or a minister may all be helpful because these individuals will usually have had some experience working with local lawyers, but will generally keep from getting too involved in the private aspects of your case.

Local lawyers who practice in a field outside of divorce, such as personal injury, bankruptcy, or corporate law, usually can target the best family lawyers in the community—and so they, too, can be excellent sources for recommendations. A good question to ask a local attorney is: "Who would you go to if you were going to get divorced?"

Of course, some people will attempt to send you to a favorite brother-in-law who just passed the bar examination or to a friend who does an occasional divorce case on the side. But keep asking for recommendations until you have at least three names. The important thing to remember as you comparison shop is that there are some excellent, ethical, and affordable divorce lawyers in your community. It's worth your time and a bit of courage to find them.

Step Two: Check Out the Local Specialists

As noted, some lawyers may advertise that they specialize in family law. In some states, this means only that this is the type of law they choose to practice; in others, it signifies that they been certified as specialists by the state bar and have passed a rigorous set of requirements. Not every case is complicated enough to require a lawyer who is a certified specialist in divorce or family law.

But if your state does certify specialists and you and your spouse are not close to any agreement on how much each of you earn, how to divide substantial assets, or how to split up any child's time with each of you, it would be a good idea to begin by at least checking out the certified specialists in your community. A specialist may charge more than you want to pay—although it will probably take him or her fewer hours to move your case along. Whatever you decide, consider this option first.

To get started, reread the information above, "What It Means to Be a Family Law Specialist." Go to the American Bar Association website on specialization at www.abanet.org/legalservices/specialization/home. html. Check out the qualifications for a specialist in family law and take a look at the explanation under the heading "For Consumers." To determine if your state lists the names of family law specialists who have met the requirements, you will need to consult the site for your state's bar association—for example, www.kentuckystatebar.org. Some states have a roster of all the certified specialists, sorted by county and specialty. If your state provides a list—as do, for example, Arizona, California, and Texas—this should be your starting base unless you know already that you don't want to pay top dollar for a lawyer.

SKIP AHEAD

If you already have names of three prospects. If you have at least three names of lawyers to interview, gathered from personal recommendations and your own sleuthing for specialists, move ahead to the next step. If you still haven't gathered enough names, you'll have to go to less reliable sources, such as the Yellow Pages and Internet advertising, discussed below.

The Yellow Pages of your phone book used to contain the only public listing of lawyers available. But lawyers seem to be decreasing their presence there these days and going for a heavier presence on the Internet. Still, many lawyers still list their specialties in the attorney section of the phone book. Look under both "divorce" and "family law" in your initial search for potential hires.

There are several Internet sites that charge lawyers a fee to carry their names and specialties. To sample them, go to a search engine and type in "Find a lawyer." You will be presented with many choices, the most established of which is at www.martindale.com, a company that has been publishing lawyer directories with ratings for competence, a hardcover book, for many years.

WARNING

Where not to look for names. Local agencies that advertise that they will refer you to a lawyer usually do not have good information about the quality of the lawyers on their lists, so it is usually wise to avoid them. The situation is better with some legal plans that offer you telephone advice from a lawyer in your state. However, if you are looking for a lawyer to represent you in all phases of your divorce, you are generally better off with someone local. And lawyers who have large display advertisements or who claim in have won golden achievement awards in the Yellow Pages are not always a good bet. I learned, for example, that a lawyer who stated he has been elected as The Best Family Lawyer in town by the readers of a local newspaper had all sorts of friends and family stuff the ballot box to secure a victory.

The Lawyer Who Had a Fool for a Client

One afternoon I was in chambers going over my files for the next day, and came across a case that looked interesting. The parties had been divorced for several years and the wife was asking for more child support because the children had grown older—and more expensive—and the husband's income had increased a great deal.

He was a lawyer in one of San Francisco's largest law firms who could easily have afforded to hire one of the best divorce lawyers in town, but decided to handle his case personally. I checked a directory of lawyers and saw he had a reputation as a skilled corporate litigator—and steeled myself for the show he'd likely put on for me and the crew of 20 or so family lawyers who would be in court to present their cases.

And what a show it was. The wife's lawyer—an experienced divorce practitioner—made a concise presentation citing cases from higher California courts on the issue at hand. Then it was the husband's turn, and he took off like a bird—confident, cheerful, and sort of persuasive. The only problem was he was trying to sell a theory that wasn't in keeping with state law. Our court conversation went something like this:

Judge (me): Mr. X, are you familiar with the case of *Marriage of Catalano* decided by the California Court of Appeal?

Mr. X: Why, no, your honor.

Me: Well, I'll ask the bailiff to go into chambers and pull that case so you can read it. We'll take another case in the meantime. Take your time and check out the current California law.

Mr. X: Thank you, your honor, I'll be happy to.

[Twenty minutes pass for the next case.]

Me: Okay, Mr. X, would like to continue your argument?

Mr. X: [Still trying to smile, but now with an embarrassed frown seeping in]: No, I don't think I'll argue that point any further, your honor, but I would like to point out one important distinction between *Catalano* and my case.

Me: Yes?

Mr. X: I never sent a limousine to pick up my son. [Low rumble of laughter from the audience, joined in quite gallantly by him.]

The lawyer lost the case—and his child support went up considerably.

Step Three: Winnow the List

Once you have a list of several potentially qualified possibilities and are sure you know what type of lawyer would best suit your needs, your next task is to winnow down your list to about three for personal interviews. If you have both certified specialists and nonspecialists on your list, include at least one of each type to interview.

Check to see if any of the lawyers on your list have their own Internet sites and search them carefully.

> **WARNING**
>
> **When location may matter.** The distance between your lawyer's office and the courthouse can be a factor for some people in some cases. Most lawyers charge for their travel time, so a lawyer whose office is in the county seat may be a better bet than one whose office is near your home.

Step Four: Interview Prospects

Call all of your finalists and tell them you are interviewing several lawyers to select someone to represent you in a divorce and that you would like to make an initial appointment for 15 to 20 minutes. Most lawyers won't charge you for a short interview while you are deciding whom you want to hire to handle your case. If you find a prospect who does charge and wants more than $100 for the interview, pass. And if a lawyer you call is too busy to take on your case, ask who he or she would recommend instead.

If you're like most people, what you are searching for is someone with whom you feel comfortable, someone who seems to be honest, smart, and understanding—and someone who understands that total victory for any one side on every issue is very rare in divorce court. You may want a lawyer with good courtroom skills to convey to your spouse's lawyer that if the case goes to trial, he or she will have a worthy adversary. But even more important, you want a lawyer with negotiating skills, whose primary goal will be to reach an amicable compromise that you will find acceptable. You also want someone who will explain all of the choices that are open to you in plain English, without using a lot of unfamiliar legal words.

TIP
Perseverance will pay. This search and winnow process sounds formidable, but the optimum qualities should not be too difficult to find. Having served in all parts of the court system and dealt with many hundreds of lawyers, I can attest that family lawyers are some of the most humane and reasonable people in the law business.

During the interview with your prospective attorneys, you should be the one asking most of the questions. Here are a few suggestions for queries you might find helpful.

- **How long have you been doing divorce law?** If it is less than a year, you should probably move along to another candidate.

- **Why did you pick this field?** Many divorce lawyers will explain thay they enjoy helping people in a difficult situation. Don't dismiss this as being unbelievable; many good lawyers choose this specialty for this very reason.

- **How many divorce cases do you usually carry at one time?** There is no good or bad answer to this question. But if the lawyer has more than 20 active cases, you are probably going to have trouble getting through to him or her on the telephone.

- **How do you bill for your time?** A good lawyer can give you a very specific answer to this question—including how he or she handles charging for travel time, bills a minimum time for phone calls—such as, a quarter of an hour even if the call is only five minutes—or bills for other office worker's time separately.

- **What out-of-pocket expenses do you normally pass along?** All lawyers will charge for fees for filing needed documents with the court and for hiring a court reporter if one is needed; some also charge for photocopying, faxes, and postage.

- **How do you feel about settling a case instead of going to trial?** The best answer is that a good settlement is better than an average trial, but you probably will pick up some clues to the lawyer's preference from this answer.

- **What percentage of your cases usually get settled?** You should probably be concerned if it is less than 80%. Someone who rattles a saber and tells you how he or she would love to embarrass your spouse on the witness stand is probably not the lawyer you are seeking.

- **Who else will be working on my case?** If there is another lawyer or paralegal in the office who will be handling substantial parts of the case, you should also meet that person.

- **How quickly do you return phone calls or email messages from a client?** When a lawyer is in trial on another case, it is possible that he or she won't be able to get back to you within a specified time. But a conscientious lawyer should be able to assure you that someone on staff will talk to you within several hours of a weekday call, and that the staffer will discuss the matter with the lawyer and get a message to you within 24 hours.

When you feel you have a pretty good picture of the character and skills of the lawyer you are interviewing, thank him or her and say you will be back in touch shortly. Don't make a decision until you have conducted all the interviews you have planned. Then make your choice.

Step Five: Get a Written Agreement

Before hiring any lawyer, be sure that he or she prepares a written agreement that each of you sign before any work is commenced. Read it over carefully. Even if you don't normally read legalistic agreements, know that this particular one is important and merits some time and effort. Ask questions about anything you don't understand. And don't hesitate to ask for a day or two to read it over at home.

The agreement should state that you have the right to terminate your relationship at any time without any penalties. There should also be a provision that if you ever decide to change lawyers, the lawyer will turn over your file to your new lawyer within no more than five days. Because most disputes between lawyers and clients are over money—that is, legal fees and costs—be sure the agreement states exactly what services you will be charged for and clearly explains hourly and any other billing rates.

⚠ **WARNING**

Know what you're getting for your money. Avoid surprises by pressing your lawyer for specifics about what he or she considers "chargeable." For example, I know a lawyer who makes a fixed charge for every time his secretary opens a file folder or sends a fax. That same lawyer hires a driver to take him to all appointments out of his office and passes the charges along to his clients.

Dealing With Your Lawyer

As with most relationships, a lawyer/client relationship is a two-way street, involving rights and responsibilities for both of you.

Your Lawyer's Duties to You

Once you agree to hire a particular lawyer, he or she is legally bound to fulfill a number of duties while representing you.

Keeping you informed. Your lawyer has the duty to keep you informed about what is happening in your case at all times. That includes getting you copies of all correspondence and pleadings filed with the court as soon as they are available. And if there are important conversations with another lawyer in the case, your lawyer should promptly relay the substance of them to you.

Abiding by your decisions. Your lawyer also has the responsibility of allowing you to make all the important decisions in the case after explaining the options to you clearly. While the lawyer can strongly recommend a particular decision, you have no obligation to take a position that is uncomfortable to you on any issue. A lawyer who is unhappy with your decision can always resign from the case.

Keeping matters confidential. Communications between a lawyer and client are protected by the attorney/client privilege and your attorney should agree to keep everything you say to him or her confidential.

Moving your case along. If getting through this difficult period quickly is important to you, you are entitled to have your case move at the pace the court system will allow—and your lawyer should let you know how long that is likely to take. If your lawyer has other cases stacked up waiting for a trial date, he or she should let you know what effect that will have on your getting to trial.

Explaining the bills. You should be given a comprehensive monthly bill with detailed charges for your lawyer's time. If there are charges you don't understand, you are entitled to an explanation.

Courteous treatment. You are entitled to be treated courteously by the lawyer and his or her staff.

If you feel your lawyer has failed to perform any of these duties, don't hesitate to act to correct the wrong. (See "If Problems Develop," below.)

Your Duties as a Client

You also have a number of duties when dealing with the individual you have hired to exercise all of his or her professional abilities to get you divorced well. Failing to fulfill these duties is sure to cost you unnecessary charges—and might even affect the outcome of your case.

Tell the truth. You have the obligation to tell your lawyer the complete truth about everything that might be relevant to your divorce—even about matters you find embarrassing. For example, if you had an affair with your boss—a fact that would normally be irrelevant in a trial—your lawyer needs to know this in advance so that he or she is not surprised if the opposing lawyer raises it in negotiations.

Respond promptly to requests. If your lawyer asks for information or documents, respond as soon as possible—and make it a high priority. Deliver any documents quickly, even if it means that you have to hound your credit card company or bank for needed information. Thousands of dollars of attorney fees are wasted when lawyers go back and forth while their clients stall in producing bank statements, copies of checks, and other items.

The High Cost of Lying

In one of the largest cases I have handled since retirement, a client told his lawyer that an antique belonging to the divorcing couple worth several hundred thousand dollars was sitting in a gallery for sale in another city. That lawyer assured the lawyer for the other spouse that it was true.

When it turned out later that the client had actually sold the work to a customer more than a year ago, his lawyer promptly resigned from the case and refused to have anything further to do with him. That client's failure to tell his lawyer the whole truth cost him a very skilled lawyer and made it difficult for him to find a reputable replacement to take over the case.

Paying your bill. Your lawyer is entitled to be paid according to whatever schedule you have agreed to for payments. If something occurs to prevent you from keeping that schedule, you should promptly inform your lawyer of the reasons for the delay in payment.

Don't be a pest. Don't pester your lawyer with minor matters about which there is little he or she can do. There are clients who phone every time a support check is a day or two late, or when a child comes back from a visit with a scraped knee. Clients who leave multiple messages about minor matters can become such irritants that the attorney ultimately seeks to avoid them.

Bear in mind that a lawyer's time is his or her stock in trade—and you will be charged for every phone call, fax, and email message sent and read on your behaf. Be aware that lawyers are often out of the office participating in depositions or appearing in court. When possible, pass essential information along by fax or email. Once you have gotten to know your lawyer's secretary, try telling him or her about information you want your lawyer to know; you won't likely be charged for the secretary's time.

Information to Provide Your Lawyer

In representing you in a divorce, your lawyer is apt to request various types of information and documents, including:

- income tax returns—including state and federal personal, corporate, and partnership returns with related W-2 and 1099 forms for at least the last three years
- income information—including payroll stubs since the filing of the last income tax return
- personal property tax returns if applicable
- banking information—including monthly statements, passbooks, check registers, canceled checks, and other records from personal and business accounts, as well as statements from certificates of deposit, money market, and retirement accounts from all institutions
- financial statements and loan applications prepared by either spouse for the last five years
- brokerage statements for all accounts of securities, commodities, or mutual funds
- stock option records
- pension, profit-sharing deferred compensation agreements, and retirement plan records and statements
- wills and trust agreements for your spouse and yourself, and
- insurance policies for life and general insurance for the past five years.

As mentioned, it can save much time and money if you are efficient in providing this documentation.

You are entitled to get information about matters that are important to you and you should not remain a client of an attorney who won't answer important questions. But maintain a perspective on what is important, so that if you are experiencing a serious pattern of harassment or threats from your spouse, your lawyer will respond promptly.

> **TIP**
> **Scratching the back that scratches yours.** When you find yourself represented by a lawyer in whom you have confidence, let him or her know that you appreciate it. Lawyers tend to do their best work for clients who respond to their requests and realize how important it is to do a divorce right.

If Problems Develop

After you have hired a lawyer to take on your case, there are some actions that can give you second thoughts about whether you made a good choice.

This may include when your lawyer:

- doesn't answer your messages within a day or two
- makes decisions about a course of action in your case without discussing it with you, or
- does not come up with specific written materials such as research assistance that you request. (See "Getting Help From an Attorney," below.)

Whatever the cause for your concern, tell your lawyer about what is bothering you as soon as possible. If you can't see him or her personally or make contact by telephone, write an email message or a letter. Explain why you feel dissatisfied with the services and see whether he or she answers your concerns.

If you don't get a satisfactory explanation, don't prolong a relationship that can cause you and your case serious problems. Start interviewing other lawyers, and when you find someone who gives you a feeling of confidence, pay a retainer, notify your former lawyer right away, and authorize your new lawyer to pick up your file from your former lawyer.

Doing Your Own Legal Research

Now that you know about when and where to get legal help from others, you might want to learn something about situations in which you may be able to improve your case by doing some legal research on your own.

Legal research can provide a leg up, for example:

- if you have a lawyer, by helping you to understand and decide on the theories and tactics of presenting your case that he or she recommends, or

- if you are going to represent yourself in at least some phases of your case, by preparing you for negotiations with your spouse or for the all-important task of planning your presentation on the law to the judge. If, for instance, you and your spouse are going to attempt to work out how much alimony one of you is going to pay the other, you should know how much might be ordered by the court if your negotiations break down and it becomes a judge's job to set the amount

Bear in mind that no sane person would play poker, tennis, or golf without knowing the rules that apply to the game. Similarly, there are very strict rules that tell judges how they must go about setting the support one spouse is ordered to pay the other, how a divorcing couple's possessions are to be divided, and various matters regarding any children involved. These laws differ from state to state.

There are two places you can find these rules:

- in the statutes—commonly called laws—passed by your state legislature, and

- in the printed opinions of the courts of your state interpreting those laws.

The judge hearing your case or approving any agreements you have reached will be considering both of these sources in making decisions that relate to your divorce.

TIP ICON
Talking like a lawyer. If you are representing yourself, you are not likely to be writing any legal briefs in your case, but you probably are going to have the opportunity to make a closing argument after the judge has heard all the evidence. It might be persuasive, for example, if you said something like this: "Your Honor, I know there are four factors you are required to consider in setting alimony. I'd like to say a few words about what the evidence has been on each of them."

And here are two ways you can locate these rules:

• by asking an attorney, or

• by doing a little research on your own.

Getting Help From an Attorney

Whether you hire an attorney to represent you completely or decide to handle your case partially or totally on your own, it can be a good idea to consult with an experienced family law attorney just to determine whether there are any legal issues that are beyond the "garden variety." (If you are hiring an attorney for just this advice on your case, see the section on "Unbundled Legal Services," above.) You should explain the financial and child custody issues of your marriage and then ask the attorney to identify the spots that could turn out to be controversial.

After you have gone over the facts, your conversation might be something like this:

Attorney: "Child custody, child support, and division of your possessions would appear to be pretty cut and dried. But the alimony could well be controversial and you might be entitled to some reimbursement for having put your husband through medical school."

You: "I'm the kind of a person who likes to understand something as important as my divorce, so even though you are going to represent me in court, I'd appreciate it if you could give me a little reading material. I'd like a photocopy of the laws of this state about how alimony is set and about whether I am entitled to something for having paid for my spouse to go through medical school. And if there are any important court decisions interpreting these laws, if you give me the citation to those cases, I'll find them and read them."

Most attorneys will be surprised—and happy—to hear your request. And most will get you the information you seek. Others might say something like: "Forget about alimony; no judge is going to give you alimony." Or: "Don't worry about the law; I'll handle that." You might well become concerned about receiving answers like those. But you can also find the relevant legal information yourself.

Going It Alone

If you don't have a lawyer, or if you have hired one but don't feel comfortable asking him or her for specific information on cases and laws, you can get the same material on your own. It just might take a bit of perseverance.

Finding Laws on the Internet

To find the law or statute you need, go to www.divorcesource.com. Click on the heading "Divorce Laws" on the left side of the page. Next click on your state, and when you get to the state page, scroll to the heading that describes the area in which you are interested—such as property division, spousal support, child custody, or child support.

As explained above, these laws, written by your state legislature, set rules and parameters for specific legal issues that may arise in a divorce. Judges are bound by this law and don't have the power to change it. So, for instance, if you and your spouse live in Texas and were married for less than ten years, the subject of spousal support is strictly limited by the controlling state statute; no support will be awarded unless the higher earner spouse was convicted of family violence within the last two years.

In some cases, it will be helpful for you to go beyond this summary and read the actual words of the state law that is being interpreted. For example, assume you live in Massachusetts and are interested in specific nuances of the law on property distribution. At the end of the section summarizing the law, there will be some brackets with titles and numbers in them: Massachusetts General Laws—Chapter 208, Sections 1A and 34, which is the reference you would use to get the state's law on property distribution.

With this information, you can find the letter of the law by going to www.nolo.com under the tab Rights & Disputes and clicking on "Go to Court or Mediate," then on "Research State Law." Then click on your state; on the introductory page, you will be asked to give either the name of the statute or a descriptive word. In this Massachusetts example, you would fill in "208" for the chapter and "34" for the section. You could also do your search by locating the "phrase" box and entering the word "alimony." In either case, you would be directed to the exact text of the Massachusetts law that sets the terms for alimony.

Finding Laws at a Law Library

If you aren't savvy about using the Internet, you can still find the laws you might need by going to a law library. There are law libraries open to the public in most big cities and all county seats. Law libraries at state and some private law schools are also often open to the public.

Find a friendly law librarian and tell him or her you need some help finding the statutes on divorce in your state. The laws you want are likely to be bound in a book that may be called the Family Code or the Civil Code or some similar title. Check out the table of contents or the index and look for the subject in which you are interested—for instance, child support or alimony, which is sometimes known as "spousal support" or "maintenance."

You should be able find what you need fairly easily. But before making copies of the laws you seek, check to see whether there is a paper pamphlet inside the back cover of the book, called the pocket part. If so, it will describe changes in the law since the date the book was published. If your law isn't listed in the pamphlet, it hasn't been amended by the legislature since the book's publication. Now take the book and, if relevant, the pamphlet, to the library's copy machine so that you can have copies of the relevant laws to review on your own time.

Finding Case Decisions Interpreting a Statute

Now you have the law your judge must apply to your case. If you have the time and the interest to go a little further, there is often additional helpful information that could be very valuable: case law.

The job of the appellate courts of your state is to apply the letter of the laws to real life people involved in a divorce in your state. These opinions are reported in decisions available in bound books in the law library and online in legal research portals.

ADDITIONAL RESOURCE

For a detailed explanation of how to do your own legal research, see *Legal Research: How to Find & Understand the Law*, by Stephen R. Elias and Susan Levinkind (Nolo). Nolo's website also offers some helpful preliminary information on research. Go to www.nolo.com; then click on "Rights and Disputes"; then "Go to Court or Mediate" and "Help with Legal Research."

If you are able to find a case that is similar to your situation, it can be very helpful in arguing your case. For example, assume that you and your spouse are battling over the issue of spousal support. And assume the statute of your state specifies that in setting alimony the judge should consider how much it would take each party "to maintain the standard of living established during the marriage." Suppose that in your marriage, the two of you always felt that putting a generous slice of your income into a savings account was an important part of your life. Now that you are getting divorced, should maintaining that practice be considered a part of your "standard of living"? Or put another way, should a wife who is going to be receiving alimony be paid enough to allow her to put several hundred dollars a month into a savings account?

If an appellate court of your state has already decided this question, it would almost certainly be useless for you to argue that a judge should rule to the contrary.

Finding important case decisions that interpret the law is a bit more complicated than finding the laws themselves. Start by digging out the numbers and words you found in the brackets at the end of the summary you find at www.divorcesource.com, or if you didn't use the Internet, the code section you found in the law library. The rather mysterious series of abbreviations and numbers is known as a citation and will look something like the Massachusetts numbers explained above. (See "Understanding Case Citations," below, for an explanation of the parts of the citation.)

For novice researchers, a law library may still be the most helpful place to begin and end a search. Show the citation to a law librarian and ask him or her where you can find a book known as "an annotated code" covering that law. That should lead you to a book that contains a little thumbnail description of cases that discuss the particular section in which you are interested. Inside the back cover of the book there probably will be a pamphlet that describes the most recent cases on the subject. If there aren't any very helpful cases in the pamphlet, go to the main bound part of the book and read the cases identified there.

Read over these descriptions, looking for something similar to the issue in your case. Don't worry if the people in the case are very different from your situation—what you are looking for is a discussion of the legal situation in the case that is similar to yours. Pick two or three of the more recent ones and copy down the little citation to the case—something like 47 Wash.2d 234 or 19 S.E.3d 345—and take it to the librarian for help in locating the volume that carries the full text of the case. Now read the full text of what the court said. If it is helpful, make a copy in the library's machine. It isn't, go on to read others until you have either found something helpful to bring up to the judge or you're too tired to go on.

Understanding Case Citations

A case citation—for example, *Smith v. Jones,* 45 A. 567 (1995)—contains a lot of important information.

First are the names of the parties separated by a "v.," which stands for "versus." The next number ("45") refers to the volume of the set of books in which the case is printed. The next letter or series of letters refers to the set of books where opinions such as this are published. The books are called reporters. A case may be published in both a state reporter (N.Y.) and a regional reporter (A. for Atlantic, N.W. for Northwest, etc.), which contains the opinions of several states. The next number (567) refers to the page on which the opinion begins in volume 45. Finally, there is a reference to the year the opinion was issued.

When Dividing Your Property, Don't Hide the Ball

For most people, splitting up your possessions is another part of the process of getting divorced. Either you and your spouse sit down and decide together who gets what—or a judge will have to divide what different states call either your "marital property" or your "community property." If possible, of course, it's best to do the dividing yourselves.

The most important advice I can give you on this subject is to be open and honest in setting out everything of value you have come to own during your marriage. That includes revealing that you still have a little bank account you stuck away secretly five years ago when the two of you were thinking about splitting up. As discussed later in this chapter, items such as these tend to surface sooner or later, and the penalties for hiding something of value can be devastating.

If you and your spouse can agree on dividing the property you own together, the court will normally approve whatever agreement you have reached. The only exception is when a party who doesn't have a lawyer seems to have agreed to take a lot less than half of the property. In that case, the judge may want to ask a few questions to be sure that one of you isn't taking advantage of the other. But don't count on this intervention in every case.

If you and your spouse can't decide how to divvy up your property on your own, it may be well worth the time and expense to hire a mediator to help with the task. (See "Going to Mediation" in Chapter 2.)

A formal agreement you reach is called a Marital Settlement Agreement and is usually prepared by a lawyer or paralegal. (See "Finalizing Your Agreement" in Chapter 2 for more on these.) But an agreement—preferably in writing—that you and your spouse have worked out without assistance should still be presented in court for whatever use the judge thinks is appropriate. If you do your own agreement, it doesn't have to have a fancy label at the top or special legalistic words within it. Just write down what you have agreed and sign at the bottom. Your agreement doesn't need to be notarized unless both parties will not be in court to verify that they agreed to its provisions. Depending on your situation, the document may be just a few paragraphs and may also be used to resolve other issues of the divorce, such as child custody, alimony, and child support.

If you can't reach an agreement on your own or with the help of a mediator or lawyers, the court will divide your property for you. But because only you and your spouse know who really cares most about that painting you bought on your honeymoon or who has pitched in the most to care for your dog over the years, a court's decision will never be as satisfactory as one that you two could prepare. In dictating the terms of a property split, the judge will be required to apply some state laws and rules that you are free to ignore if you reach your own agreement. In some states, for example, a judge could decide that one of you was guilty of "marital fault," so instead of dividing the property by a normal 50/50 split, it should be divided 70/30. And the one who gets 30% may be you.

If you only have a few items of property to be divided, the judge may make the division personally, perhaps ordering some property to be sold so that there are enough liquid assets to make an equal division. But if there are a lot of items to be divided, the judge may appoint a lawyer or appraiser as a "referee" to evaluate the property and propose a division for the judge to approve. The parties are usually ordered to pay the referee's expense.

As you read this chapter, keep in mind that the term "property" does not refer only to real estate. It also encompasses what the law calls "personal property"—which includes possessions such as your clothes, the family dog, bank accounts, furniture, investments, pensions, and the manuscript of the book you have been writing for the past six years.

No matter how amicable things may be between you and your soon-to-be-ex, try to get everything you have agreed to in writing as soon as possible. Having a clear written agreement about who owns what after you and your spouse split can avoid disputes that sometimes occur later about just what you agreed to when you separated. And having this property agreement incorporated into your divorce judgment makes it easier to enforce.

Judges Don't Do Windows, Either

One of the first large divorces I handled when I was a young(ish) lawyer involved a well-to-do middle-aged cardiologist and his wife.

The couple had a house full of beautiful things that the opposing lawyer and I had listed on an inventory that was several pages long. Many of the more expensive items had been wedding presents and there were little notes about who had given the present and whether it had been intended as a gift to one of them or jointly to both. We handed it all to the judge and naively expected him to do the division.

He glanced at it quickly, chuckled quietly, and said, "Counsel, I'm sorry, but the court does not do silverware."

After the parties heard it would cost them several thousand dollars to have a neutral referee evaluate and divide the items, they figured out a way to do it themselves.

The High Cost of Hiding the Ball

The rest of this chapter outlines the legal mechanics of dividing up your possessions, but first I want to again underscore an essential point: When splitting up your property, don't hide the ball.

Hiding assets from a spouse during divorce is not only a devious thing to do, it's illegal. The law provides that married people have a legal relationship known as a "fiduciary duty" from the time they get married until at least the moment when they are finally divorced. This duty, the highest standard of trust and confidence recognized by the law, continues through a period of marital separation and, in many cases, until your possessions are finally physically divided.

If you violate this duty and hide some asset, your spouse may get tipped off by sources you would never imagine: a piece of junk mail that somehow gets forwarded, the bank statement you mistakenly left in that jacket that was going to the cleaners, or a disgruntled former employee who wants to get even for some slight that occurred on the job.

Of Lawyers and Liars

When I was a lawyer, I learned belatedly the importance of protecting myself from taking on a client who told less than the whole truth.

I'd only been practicing law for a year when a friend sent me a client: her well-to-do father, gearing up for a hotly contested divorce. He told me that he had owned a very valuable ring long before his marriage and that his wife clearly had no right to any portion of it. When I told his wife's lawyer our position on the ring, she smiled and said something about my being young and trusting and that she'd have some surprises for me at trial.

At the trial, she waited for my client to make his claim, and on cross-examination showed him an invoice from a jewelry store dated two years after the couple was married for a diamond ring that matched the ring in evidence. The husband hotly denied the validity of the invoice, but before long the jeweler who had sold it to him showed up in court and was on the witness stand and testifying that my client had lied.

A kindly judge recessed the hearing and invited the two lawyers into his chambers. He said he could tell my client had duped me, and that if I wanted permission to remove myself from the case, he would allow it and continue the case for my client to find a new lawyer.

I thanked him, told my client what had happened—and left the courthouse.

Legal Repercussions

If you are caught hiding the ball, a court is almost sure to order you to pay the fees and expenses your ex-spouse incurs in litigating the issue. You can be forced to forfeit the entire disputed item as a penalty for lying.

And your loss may include more than money alone: Your creditability with the court will be pretty well shot. As a result, the judge might decide not to believe any of your testimony on disputed items. After all, if you were willing to lie under oath in court about one matter, why should you be believed on others?

And finally, when your lawyer learns that you have not told the truth about an important legal matter, he or she may resign from the case. If you seek to hire another lawyer, he or she will want to know what happened with your former lawyer—and may even insist on having a conversation with that lawyer to investigate.

Tips on Finding Hidden Assets

If you suspect that your spouse may be hiding a ball or two, here are some suggestions about how to dig for additional information.

- If you have access to a jointly owned computer that your spouse has used at any time in the past, consider hiring an expert to explore the recesses of the computer's memory.

- If the two of you had any joint financial accounts, talk with representatives at the financial institution about what it would require for you to get copies of cancelled checks and records of transfers of funds. A lawyer could also accomplish this through a formal legal process called discovery, but if your name is on the account, you can usually do it on your own much more easily and inexpensively.

- If your spouse worked for an employer that might have provided a pension during your marriage, contact the company for any information that you are entitled to learn about.

- If you don't have copies of past income tax returns, get them from the IRS and hire an accountant to see if there any leads to hidden investments.

ADDITIONAL RESOURCES
A book that provides helpful information on locating hidden assets directly through a tax form is *The 1040 Handbook: A Guide to Income Discovery*, by Jack Zuckerman and others (American Bar Association, Section of Family Law). And many additional tips on locating a spouse's hidden property in general are covered in *Divorce & Money: How to Make the Best Financial Decisions During Divorce*, by Violet Woodhouse and Dale Fetherling (Nolo).

Cases in Point: The High Price of Hiding Assets

Three recent cases point up the perils of hiding assets from a soon-to-be former spouse while divorcing.

The $1 million junk mail case. This case got started when the wife, who was contemplating divorce after 25 years of marriage, received notice that she was entitled to a $1.3 million lottery jackpot from a ticket purchased through a pool at her workplace. She claims that when she told workers at the Lottery Commission about her marital malaise, they suggested she file for divorce before she got her first check of $66,800 less taxes. Shortly thereafter, she filed, but never told her husband about her prize, and used her mother's address to receive checks and other information from the lottery.

About two years later, a letter addressed to the ex-wife mistakenly arrived at the former husband's home. He opened the letter and found that it asked if she was interested in a lump-sum buyout of the lottery proceeds she was receiving in annual installments. He quickly hired a lawyer to file a motion asking the court to reopen the divorce proceedings and, because of her breach of her duty to reveal all of her possessions in the divorce, he also asked to be awarded 100% of the winnings. The court gave him just that. (*In re Marriage of Rossi*, 90 Cal. App. 4th 34 (2001).)

The case of the fiduciary breacher. In this case, the wife discovered that when she and her husband divorced, he failed to reveal that he had a claim for a 25% interest in recordings he had produced for the legendary deceased guitarist Jimi Hendrix. In his testimony in a 45-minute trial in divorce court, he had stated under oath that he had no ownership interest in Hendrix's estate or in Are You Experienced? Ltd., the company that marketed Hendrix's works.

In a new trial five years later, the court found that although there was no evidence the husband had received anything after the divorce due to his arrangement with Hendrix, he had violated his fiduciary duty to inform the wife during their divorce proceedings that he had a pending claim for an interest in the Hendrix estate. The husband was ordered to pay almost $150,000 for her attorney fees in pursuing her claim. In addition, he revealed in a document filed with the court, it had cost him $495,300 in attorney fees to defend himself on these charges. (*Rubenstein v. Rubenstein*, 2006 Cal. App. Unpub LEXIS 776.)

The exposed hider who just kept hiding. I was involved in this case after my retirement, serving as a discovery referee. Judges sometimes appoint such referees to handle complicated portions of a case to save court time. The husband and wife owned a number of valuable works of art, some of which they divided between themselves as part of their divorce. However, one of the pieces—for which they had paid $40,000— appreciated to be worth several hundred thousand dollars. The couple agreed it should be sold by an independent dealer they both trusted, and that the proceeds should then be divided equally.

The husband had the painting, and quickly began an intricate game of hide-the-ball. First he secretly sold the painting and pocketed the proceeds. When the wife became curious about the painting's whereabouts, he was forced to reveal what he had done. Eventually he produced a false invoice showing a sales price of $250,000. Many court hearings and a trip to the appellate court later, he was forced to disclose that he had actually sold it for $425,000. Further hearings revealed there had been several more unreported sales of the couple's paintings, netting him more than $400,000. My recommendation was that the ball hider should pay 100% of the proceeds of all these sales to the wife. Absent his lies, she would have been entitled to only half. The trial judge agreed.

In addition to losing all proceeds from the sales of the paintings, the husband has been ordered to pay the wife attorney fees and sanctions totaling more than a million dollars. He has almost certainly paid more than that for the fees of his own lawyers, plus half of my fees as referee. His total costs for hiding the ball will probably be several million dollars.

Laws on Dividing Property

There are two general legal theories used in the United States for dividing marital possessions at divorce. The community property method is used in Arizona, California, Idaho, Louisiana, New Mexico, Nevada, Texas, Washington, and Wisconsin—and also in Alaska, if the spouses agree in writing. The equitable distribution method is used in the other states.

The basic concept of the community property theory is that all of the property the spouses own is divided equally. The concept of the equitable distribution theory is that the couple's property is divided equitably, which means fairly. At first glance, you might think there is a big difference between the two concepts. However, in application, they are not that different.

A careful look at the laws of the community property states reveals that only three of them—California, Louisiana, and New Mexico—stick stubbornly to the requirement of an equal division. The other community property states insist on an equal division "unless it would be inequitable to do so." And the decision of whether it would be inequitable is left up to the judge who tries the case.

In equitable distribution states, a judge almost always starts with an assumption that the property will be divided equally, but may depart from that if either you or your lawyer make a convincing argument it would be inequitable or unfair not to do so.

The bottom line: A divorcing couple's property will always be divided equally in California, Louisiana, and New Mexico. And it normally will be divided equally in other states, but may be divided differently if a judge decides fairness requires it.

> **TIP**
> **Squaring fairness with wiggle room.** Chapter 4 warns that you shouldn't count on courts delivering fairness in your case. And that is true. However, in some community property states and in all the equitable distribution states, the state legislatures have given judges an opportunity to depart from dividing property equally where not doing so would be unfair. I call this opportunity the "Wiggle Room," and discuss it in some detail below.

In dealing with property acquired during a marriage, it doesn't matter which spouse earned the money in the bank accounts. If it was earned during the marriage, it belongs to the parties jointly. So, for example, if a corporation president gets a $1 million bonus during a marriage and deposits it in a bank account in his or her name alone, the other spouse will normally get half of what is left of the bonus when the couple separates and divorces. In equitable distribution states, this property is called "marital property." In community property states, it is called "community property."

The Wiggle Room

In the attempt to avoid the perceived unfairness of an equal split of property where one spouse has outdone the other in giving to or taking from the marriage, the legislatures of most states have created a long list of factors that may be considered when making the division.

These factors give the judges some "Wiggle Room" in avoiding an equal division where they feel it would be inappropriate. Some states end their list of factors by adding a catch-all wiggle—that is, in addition to the list of factors, the property need not be divided equally "where it would be inequitable or inappropriate to do so given the circumstances of the case."

New York law puts it this way: "The court shall consider...any other factor which [it] shall expressly find to be just and proper. In any action in which the court shall determine that an equitable distribution is appropriate but would be impractical or burdensome..., the court in lieu of such equitable distribution shall make a distributive award in order to achieve equity between the parties." That's a lot of wiggle. Judges don't use it often, but it may be something you want to lobby for in your case.

If you have hired an experienced lawyer to help with your divorce, he or she should be able to quickly recite any Wiggle Room factors in your state and let you know how often the local judges depart from equality. Most mediators will be able to do the same thing.

You can also get a quick summary of the controlling law by going on the Internet to www.divorcesource.com and clicking on "Divorce Laws" on the left side of the page, and then your state. Once on the screen summarizing your state's law, scroll down to "Property Distribution."

If you prefer, you can check out the letter of your state's law yourself. (See "Doing Your Own Legal Research" in Chapter 5.) In doing this, you can come up with the exact language of the controlling law.

Some of the factors that states have adopted are:

- the duration of the marriage
- each spouse's contribution to the marriage, including contributions to the care and education of the children and services as homemaker
- any interruption of the careers or educational opportunities of either spouse
- one spouse's contributions to the other's career or education
- the desirability of retaining any asset—including an interest in a business, corporation, or professional practice—intact and free from any claim or interference by the other person
- the intentional dissipation, waste, depletion, or destruction of marital assets
- the value of each spouse's separate property, and
- the desirability of retaining the marital home as a residence for any dependent child of the marriage or any other person.

At one time, many states included the concept of marital fault as one of the factors to be considered. Adultery, desertion, and cruelty were some of the behaviors that were deemed to be "fault." Fault, particularly domestic violence, is still included in many state laws as a factor to be considered in setting alimony, but many others now clearly indicate that fault—including adultery and cruelty—should not be considered in dividing property.

The Wiggle Room Explored

The use of Wiggle Room was explored and debated in a case recently decided by a court in Florida.

The wife had asked the trial court to make what she said was an equitable, rather than equal, distribution of a 401(k) plan. To bolster her argument, she claimed that during the marriage she had been frugal and thrifty, while her husband fished and played racquetball. She also pointed to the fact that he left the marriage "without any attempt at marriage counseling."

The trial court agreed with her and ordered the 401(k) plan divided 75% to the wife and 25% to the husband.

However, the appellate court ordered an equal distribution. It noted that one party's misconduct was not generally considered a basis for unequal distribution unless it adversely affected the financial status of the other party.

The dissenting justice scolded the other justices for "restricting the trial court's discretion" and having "taken one step further to judicially legislate distribution of assets be 'equal' rather than 'equitable.'" (*Horne v. Horne*, 711 So. 2d 1310, 1313 (1998).)

Note that although the wife in this case lost her attempt to get a wiggle, she did have the votes of the trial judge and one appellate justice. Equitable distribution is not dead.

Property That Won't Be Divided

Many marriages also include some property that does not fall into the category discussed above. It is called "nonmarital property" in equitable division states and "separate property" in community property states.

Nonmarital property generally consists of:

- **property that a spouse owned individually before the marriage.** For example, if yours is a second marriage, it may include property you agreed to take or were awarded by the court in your previous marriage. An asset acquired in exchange for preowned assets retains the same character. For example, assume that you owned a house you lived in before your second marriage and sold it after being married for some years, investing the proceeds in a new house. In most states, you would have a good argument that at least a portion of the proceeds of the new house is nonmarital property. And income from nonmarital assets such as rents from a tenant who lives in a house that is nonmarital property is normally also excluded from the property division laws at divorce.

- **gifts given to a spouse either before or during a marriage.** If your parents gave you a check on your birthday, for example, it will normally be considered separate property—that is, unless the card that came with it said it was given to both you and your spouse, in which case it belongs in the other category. And a writing is not necessary to prove the nature of the gift if there is other evidence of their intentions, including perhaps their testimony in court.

- **inheritances.** This is money or property one spouse received upon the death of a friend or relative and kept separate from the couple's joint accounts.

Tracing separate or nonmarital property once its title—that is, the owner listed on a bank account or on a deed to property—is changed to joint tenancy ("Barbara Johnson and Scott Johnson, as joint tenants"), or it is mixed into a community or marital account, can be quite complicated. State laws vary on whether property can recover its separate character after such an event, but frequently it cannot. In tracing such property, the records of old bank accounts and the checks must sometimes be obtained from financial institutions at considerable expense.

If a party keeps separate or nonmarital property in his or her own name, it is almost always awarded to that person. There are a few exceptions in several states; you can find them by checking the exact law in your state. (See "Doing Your Own Legal Research" in Chapter 5 for help with this.)

TIP

What goes in your account stays in your account. The bottom line is that if you have property you brought into the marriage or received as a gift or an inheritance during the marriage, it remains yours alone unless you get careless—or generous—about the labels on the accounts in which it is kept.

And Who Owns the Bills?

The responsibility for who must pay the bills that either spouse incurred before marriage or after the parties have separated can also raise questions at divorce.

Generally, bills that one spouse individually incurred before marriage are the responsibility of the one who created the debt. But any debt incurred during marriage by either spouse is a joint obligation.

Some states provide that the joint responsibility ends when the parties begin to live apart. But if your spouse runs up debt after the two of you separate, you can still be liable if you signed his or her application for a credit card or charge account. Canceling joint accounts is an important protection against having to pay for your divorcing spouse's purchases.

As discussed above, marital or community property—both the assets and the liabilities—is generally divided equally at divorce. But that doesn't mean that the most valuable items need to be converted to cash and then split. Instead, the pluses and minuses of the assets—which may include one of the spouses taking the family house at its appraised net value—and debts assigned to each party are calculated.

To make an equal division, the difference between all that is awarded to each spouse is divided in half and the one with the larger share pays the one with the smaller share. This "equalizing payment" will usually be calculated to be paid by the spouse with the greater share to the other spouse within a specified period, sometimes with a recorded lien to secure the payment. For example, if all of the assets awarded to the husband add up to $10,000 and those awarded to the wife are valued at $12,000, the wife would owe the husband an equalizing payment of $1,000.

Dividing Your Own Property

As explained earlier, in all states but California, Louisiana, and New Mexico—which strictly require an equal property division at divorce—if you take the issue of dividing your property to court, the judge can divide it any way he or she thinks is fair.

And the judge's picture of what is fair will necessarily be based on some fairly brief testimony from you and your spouse on what took place between the two of you during your marriage. It would be very difficult for anyone to get an accurate picture of your married life this way. Most of the time, the judge hearing your case will probably decide to divide it by some objective idea of what is equal, but there is just no way to be sure.

And except in the three states identified above, a judge may decide to divide your property unequally. For example, he or she may award the car you love and have been driving for years to your spouse. Not to mention what might happen to your dog.

All of the wiggle factors discussed above make it very difficult to predict how a trial before a judge will come out. In deciding how to divide the marital property, will the judge be impressed by a mother's hard work in raising a disabled child and reward her appropriately? Will the father's huge bonuses providing for a lavish lifestyle be considered an important factor? The result may well depend on which of several judges is assigned to decide your case. And, despite what you read in Chapter 4 about how limited judges are in interpreting certain laws, they are pretty free to indulge their personal predilections in this field.

The only way you can avoid the uncertainty of giving the decision making to a judge is to reach an agreement with your spouse on how the property will be divided. (See Chapter 2 for a full discussion of the available methods for reaching such agreements out of court.)

If you use a third person such as a mediator to help divide your possessions, he or she will likely suggest a method for how to proceed.

First Steps

If you and your spouse are going to try to divide your property yourselves, here are some steps to get you started.

List your belongings. Working together, make a list of all of the items that you own jointly and need to be divided. Of course, you can omit items both of you agree are personal things of insignificant value. And, for example, when dealing with furniture that is not of great value, you can just specify "furniture in master bedroom," "dining room furniture," and so on.

Value the property. Try to agree on the value of anything worth more than a specific agreed amount—say $100 or $500. If there is a house, a business, or anything that is difficult to value, get an opinion about that from some agreed outside authority. For example, for your house, pick a realtor who is familiar with your neighborhood. Or you can hire a professional appraiser for antiques. You may need an actuary to value a pension and an accountant to help you value an investment. If there is a mortgage or other debt associated with any item, be sure to subtract the amount of the debt from its value so that you list its net value.

> **WARNING**
>
> **One expert is best.** Try very hard to agree on one person to hire as an outside expert for appraising your particular property values: for real estate, the same professional real estate appraiser; for pensions, one actuary; for art, a respected dealer. I have seen some very hostile parties waste a lot of time and money by causing as many as six different appraisers to testify at a trial.

Decide the logical owner. Now go through your main list, item by item, and decide whether there is some good reason to have each piece of property go to one or the other of you. Start with the items with the biggest value and see how far you can get. If having an equal split is important to you, keep track of the total value each person accumulates. Later, trade off on the smaller items, with each of you taking one in turn.

Additional Techniques

If it becomes difficult to proceed as suggested above, it may be helpful to try a few additional methods.

Coin flip I. Flip a coin and have the winner divide up all the items you and your spouse must divvy up into two lists. Do not break up sets of things, such as dishes and tables with matching chairs. The loser of the coin flip then chooses which list he or she will take; the remaining list belongs to the listmaker.

Coin flip II. Flip a coin and have the winner place a monetary value on each item on a list of items to be divided. The other person then chooses the items he or she wants, up to one-half of the total value of all the items on the list. The person who won the flip is awarded what remains. This method can also be used for one item at a time: The first person places a value on an item, such as the car, and the other person either takes it at that value, or it goes to the first person at that value.

Hold a sale. Hold a garage sale, then divide the proceeds equally.

Entertain bids. On items of substantial value—a house, a business, an expensive car—have each spouse submit a sealed bid; when the bids are opened, the highest bidder gets the item. An equalizing payment, as described above, is made at the end of the process. For example, if you have an expensive antique and one of you bids $8,000 and the other $9,000 on it, the higher bidder gets the item at its listed value.

Auction it off. Hold a real auction with a neutral person acting as auctioneer and the two spouses being the only bidders allowed. Any increased bids should be a minimum percentage, such as 5%, over the last bid. Otherwise, the parties might be able to force the proceedings to go on into the night as they raised one another a dollar at a time.

Special Rules for Some Property

The laws in many states have special rules that apply to dividing a few types of property at divorce—including professional degrees, personal injury awards, and appreciated businesses.

Professional degrees. Many states have specific laws for dealing with a professional degree earned during the marriage, particularly if one spouse made financial sacrifices for the other spouse's education. For example, some laws provide that the spouse who earned the degree must reimburse the other for out-of-pocket expenses, such as tuition and books. Others simply factor in contributions to education and training when dividing marital property. (To find out the specifics in your state laws, follow the directions in "Doing Your Own Legal Research" in Chapter 5.)

Personal injury awards. A personal injury award is a sum of money paid to a person who is injured by the party who is responsible for causing the injury. There are special rules for how to divide money received for a personal injury award to one of the spouses. If some of the award is based upon the pain and suffering or permanent injury of the spouse involved in the accident, a good argument can be made that this portion of the award need not be shared with the other spouse. On the other hand, that portion of the award attributable to wage loss or diminishing of affection and sexual relations might well be divided.

Appreciated businesses. Most states have rules for how to divide the increase in value during the marriage of a business one of the spouses owned before the marriage took place. For example, if the business increases in value after marriage and then later is sold, the portion of the sales price that is attributable to the efforts of the business owner after marriage is normally marital or community property. Any portion that is based on its value before marriage and natural growth, not attributable to the owner's efforts, is properly nonmarital or separate property.

> **SEE AN EXPERT**
>
> **Some property division requires expert advice.** Consider consulting a lawyer for advice in dividing the following types of property: pensions, life insurance policies, stock in closely held companies, and property that has changed in its legal character because of the investment of marital property into a nonmarital asset, or vice versa.

Putting It in Writing

Once you and your spouse agree on how to divide your property, you will need to put that agreement in writing so that it can be legally enforced—and combine it with the other agreements you have reached, such as the amount of alimony or child support to be paid. (See Chapters 7 and 8.)

If you are not using a lawyer to help with this aspect of your case, when you finally appear in court for the divorce, have several copies of a neatly typed list of what each of you are taking and ask the judge to incorporate it in the judgment. If you have a lawyer, he or she will take care of having it incorporated.

In a short marriage in which there are just a few items of relatively little value that have already been divided up, this can be accomplished by a simple sentence in a judgment or an informal settlement agreement signed by both spouses. It can state something general, such as: "Each of the parties is to have as their separate property all of the items and property presently in their possession."

> **TIP**
>
> **Picture this—if you fear a later disagreement.** If you want to be extra careful, have a friend take and date a photograph of what you possess after the division has taken place. It is better to have someone else do this documentation rather than to do it yourself because if some disagreement occurs in the future, that person could testify in court in support of your position. Otherwise, a later dispute over who has the property could easily turn into a battle of He Said, She Said.

If you have more property than could reasonably be dealt with in a short agreement, or you simply prefer to list your property items, add an introduction to the list, such as: "Shirley Jones and Ralph Jones are in the process of getting divorced. As part of that process, they met on April 5, 20xx to divide the property of their marriage. After negotiations, they agreed that the following items are to immediately become the separate property or separate obligation of the party under whose name it is listed."

SEE AN EXPERT

If your situation is less than simple. Short agreements such as those discussed above may be used in relatively simple, uncomplicated cases, but they are not advisable for more complicated ones. If you are willing and able to afford a lawyer for only one aspect of your divorce, this may be the wisest place to invest.

Some thornier questions that might arise include: If the IRS audits a past income tax return you filed jointly and finds payments and penalties are due, whose responsibility is it to pay? If one of you hits upon hard times and files in bankruptcy, should they give you the opportunity to join them and thus avoid the creditors coming after you? If there is an alimony provision, should the party receiving payments be protected by life insurance if the paying party dies prematurely? Should there be a similar provision regarding child support? These are questions a lawyer and your property division agreement might well address.

CHAPTER

7

Don't Waste Time
Fighting Alimony

You'll have to deal with reality: Alimony—a monthly support payment one divorced spouse pays the other—is a living, breathing part of the American divorce system. And to get through this divorce of yours, whether you are male or female, you are much better off accepting the fact that if you earn substantially more money than a spouse to whom you have been married for several years, there is a good chance you will be ordered to pay him or her some alimony.

If alimony is ordered, you will generally have to pay a specified amount each month until:

- a date set by a judge several years in the future

- your former spouse remarries

- your children no longer need a full-time parent at home

- a judge determines that after a reasonable period of time, your spouse has not made a sufficient effort to become at least partially self-supporting

- some other significant event, such as retirement, occurs—convincing a judge to modify the amount paid, or

- one of you dies.

As with most issues in your divorce, you and your spouse can agree to the amount and length of time alimony will be paid. But if you can't agree, a court will set the terms for you. Unfortunately, as this chapter explains, having a court make the decision means there will be a trial on the issue, and that can cost you a lot of time and money.

If you expect to pay alimony. The fact you have to pay alimony—also known in some states as "spousal support" or "maintenance"—to your ex-spouse doesn't amount to a finding that you are a bad person. Consider it part of the cost for entering a marriage that you probably thought would last until death parted you, but—for reasons you didn't anticipate—didn't. It has been the law for more than 100 years and there is no sign of it being abolished. However, its use is declining somewhat.

If you expect to receive alimony. "Alimony drones" who sit and pop bonbons while watching television or playing bridge all day are pretty much a thing of the past. The question of whether you qualify for alimony is usually resolved by looking at your capacity to earn—which is not necessarily what you are earning at the time you go to court—how much your spouse earns, and your standard of living during the marriage.

You might also be required to make some changes in your life and work. For example, if you have a part-time job that doesn't pay well, you may be required to attempt to find full-time employment in a better-paid field based on the court's evaluation of your earning capacity. Experts called vocational evaluators are sometimes hired to report to the court on the job prospects for a spouse who hasn't been fully employed. The evaluator will administer vocational tests and then shop your credentials with potential employers.

RESOURCES

For more advice on how alimony payments might fit into your total financial picture, see *Divorce & Money: How to Make the Best Financial Decisions During Divorce*, by Violet Woodhouse and Dale Fetherling (Nolo).

A Brief Look at Alimony's Underpinnings

Alimony's roots probably go back to around 800 A.D. when a custom developed that at marriage, the bride's parents gave the groom a dowry—money and property considered to be all her worldly goods—in return for his promise to assume the duty to care for and support her for life.

Fifty years ago, most former spouses—usually wives—received some alimony. Today, it's not a given in every case. But thousands of years after alimony originated, every state still has a law allowing judges to order it under some circumstances.

Whether you expect to pay alimony or receive it, you need to find out what the law of your state is and how it applies to you. (See "State Law Differences," below, and "Doing Your Own Legal Research" in Chapter 5 for more detail on this.) And if you secure an alimony order, but your spouse refuses to make the required payments, take immediate legal action. (See "Violations of Alimony Orders" in Chapter 10.)

FAST FORWARD

You can skip the rest of the chapter and go on to the next if:

- You and your spouse have agreed that neither one of you is interested in paying or receiving alimony. A surprisingly large number of people fit into this category. As more women are snagging better-paying jobs, many of them don't need or want alimony—some because they favor a clean break with as few economic ties to a former spouse as possible.

- You and your spouse have agreed that one of you will pay alimony to the other in a particular amount for either a limited or unlimited time—and you don't care about what the law would say about what alimony should be. In other words, it's just the way you want to do it.

- Your marriage lasted a relatively short period—say, two years or less—and neither of you is physically or mentally disabled. In such cases, except for a brief period of "rehabilitation," alimony is very unlikely.

- You and your spouse are both in good health, of relatively equal age—within five years or so—and your incomes are about the same. Unless there are some special circumstances, this is not the kind of situation in which alimony is likely. If you were married for at least ten years or so, the court may reserve your right to request alimony in the future if you were to become disabled and your ability to work were to fold up unexpectedly.

Attitudes That Hurt

Excited statements are often uttered in and around divorce courtrooms, including:

- "I don't care how much support I have to pay for the kids, but I'm not paying that bitch [or bastard] a dime for alimony."
- "That judge can order me to pay alimony, but I know some places in this world where they'll play hell to find me."
- "I am going to hit him up for so much alimony that he'll need three jobs just to keep up the payments."
- "If I pay my ex any support, I want the court to order that I get an accounting every month on just how my money was spent."

I often used to hear statements like these from lawyers who wanted me to know their client's moods, from the court bailiffs who heard it from people sitting in the audience while waiting for their cases to be called—and, once in a while, from a straight-shooter standing before the bench without a lawyer and letting me have a piece of his or her mind.

Statements like these damage your chances for settlement, hurt your image with the judge who is going to be making your alimony order, and demonstrate a serious misunderstanding of reality. Of course, many people feel anger and frustration when confronted with the fact that they are going to have to pay alimony to a spouse with whom they no longer share a pillow. And if you are expecting to receive rather than pay alimony, it is perfectly normal to feel severe angst over the fact that the amount being proposed will result in seriously lowering your lifestyle.

It is wise to remember that whether you have the potential of paying or receiving alimony, histrionics won't help your case. (See Chapter 11 for a discussion of moving on with your life after a divorce.)

Keeping Up With the Times

As mentioned, the frequency of alimony orders has decreased as the role of women in the workworld has improved and the number of stay-at-home moms has decreased. And, although they are still not in the majority, the number of men who are receiving alimony from their higher-earning former wives has multiplied to the point that it is no longer remarkable.

The growth of the concept of "the disposable marriage" hasn't helped alimony's public image. For example, back when I was growing up, I can't recall any of my parents' friends getting divorced. And when I first began practicing law in the early 60s, people who were seeking a divorce frequently appeared almost apologetic; they seemed a bit embarrassed that they had given up on their marriage and hadn't been able to solve their mutual problems. Divorce was considered slightly scandalous. But by the late 60s, that concept changed. Potential divorce clients who came to my law office usually didn't want to talk about reconciliation or marriage counseling. They wanted to toss away their failed marriages and move on with their lives.

And for many, that attitude has persisted. Some Americans now seem to feel that if their marriages become boring, they should be able to shed them as easily as they discard a five-year-old computer. When they hear about alimony, some people realize for the first time that their marriages are not quite so easily tossed. At the same time that we hear from husbands-in-a-hurry anxious to start their new lives, we still see plenty of bright middle-aged stay-at-home moms come to court describing the career opportunities they gave up—with their husband's full agreement—to make a good home and raise the couple's children. "We made a lot of plans for the future when we got married and now he wants to leave the kids and me behind and pretend we don't exist," a wife of this stripe will say. "He shouldn't be allowed to escape his financial obligations."

The High Cost of Going to Trial

In many cases involving alimony awards, the parties agree between themselves—sometimes with the help of a mediator—on how much alimony would be "fair." In other cases, they are advised by lawyers, who predict for them what the courts are likely to do if their case goes to trial—and often, that spurs them to reach an agreement.

If you are working with a lawyer and reach agreement on alimony, he or she will formalize what you have agreed to in a Marital Settlement Agreement. It will be presented to the court at the appropriate time and incorporated in the final divorce judgment. If you and your spouse agree between yourselves on the appropriate alimony amount, you should add that to your final written agreement. (See "Finalizing Your Agreement" in Chapter 2.) As discussed below, you can also agree to waive alimony if you choose—but note that the decision may be irreversible.

There are, of course, plenty of cases in which spouses can't reach an agreement on alimony. In these cases, a judge has to conduct a trial to make the final decision on who must pay alimony and for how long. Sometimes these trials last 20 minutes; others go on for a week or more. The sad thing about some of the longer ones is that they are often a waste of time and money because their significant facts are so clear and undisputed that the decision could have been made just as well before the trial as after it.

Often the person who objects to paying isn't really fighting over the terms of an alimony order. The actual matter at issue is the fervent belief that the concept of alimony has outlived its useful life in modern times and that it should not be awarded, regardless of the circumstances. The person being asked to pay alimony—usually the husband, but not always—simply instructs his or her lawyer to contest every fact that goes into an award of alimony and to call every witness who might be able to present helpful testimony on the issue. Judges are limited in what they can do to shorten a trial in which one of the parties has a long list of witnesses and documents that he or she insists on presenting.

As a result, alimony trials often consist of hours on end of dueling certified public accountants explaining how some benefits the husband received from his employer should be evaluated in calculating his "real income." And there may also be dueling vocational evaluators explaining what one spouse's prospects are for obtaining gainful employment. Other experts might examine the parties' estimated postdivorce costs of living. And perhaps a psychologist or two will testify about whether it is in the interests of the children to have the wife or husband discontinue staying at home and go out to obtain employment. All of these potential witnesses have their depositions taken as part of the preparation for trial. Such trials are long and expensive. Two lawyers, six dueling experts sitting first for a deposition, and then a trial could easily cost the divorcing parties more than $50,000 each.

Image Consultants Prompt a Name Change

Comedians and commentators have made alimony the butt of so many jokes about beleaguered husbands that the name now belongs in same box as root canals. Starting in California in 1980, there was a movement to change alimony's reputation by giving it a new name: spousal support.

The newer-fangled term still defines payments from the higher earning spouse to the lower earning spouse, but its name change accompanied other major changes in the divorce laws of many states. As coeditor Stephen D. Sugarman notes in the book, *Divorce Reform at the Crossroads*, the name change seemed designed to call attention to the fact that beginning in the 1960s, substantial reform was occurring in the American way of divorce and alimony was being awarded in a new context.

This book uses the term alimony, but if you live in a state in which the concept has gained a little more respectability by acquiring a new name, you'll want to call it by its new moniker, often "spousal support," "maintenance," or "compensatory payments."

The Alimony Amount

In comparison to child custody cases—in which judges must decide which parent a child is going to live with—deciding on an alimony amount is a piece of cake. Every state has a law dictating what factors must be considered in setting alimony. (See the discussion below, "State Law Differences," for specifics on the law controlling your situation.)

Basically, in setting the amount of alimony to be paid, courts look at:

• how much money each person could reasonably earn every month

• what the reasonable expenses are going to be for each of them, and

• whether an alimony award from one to the other would make it possible for each to go forward with a lifestyle somewhat close to what the couple had before they split—known in divorce law as "the standard of living established during the marriage."

As is frequently the case, if there isn't enough money to make it possible for the parties to reestablish something close to their marital standard of living, then most judges will look for a way to make the divorcing parties share the financial pain equally.

EXAMPLE: Here's how the math works out in a typical alimony case. Imagine that a husband who files for divorce earns $5,000 a month. His wife stays at home with three young children and earns no income. Under their state's formula, she's entitled to $1,650 child support per month. But say she convinces the judge that her total rock bottom needs, including a house payment, are $2,300. If the judge is convinced her budget is solid and that her husband can afford it, she would be awarded $650 in spousal support: $2,300 minus $1,650. (For more on a judge's discretion in these decisions, see "My 40% Rule," below.)

Are Savings Included in a Standard of Living?

In many states, the law specifies that in setting alimony, the judge should consider how much support it would take each party "to maintain the standard of living established during the marriage." This can raise questions about how a court should set and evaluate a particular standard within the "standard of living."

For example, consider the married couple who agreed that it was important to put a generous slice of their income in a savings account. Now that they are getting divorced, should that practice be considered a part of their standard of living? Courts in California, North Carolina, Virginia, and Wisconsin have answered that question in the affirmative. Courts in Florida and Hawaii have found to the contrary.

In one of the California decisions, the court noted: "We fail to see why Wife should be deprived of her accustomed lifestyle just because it involved the purchase of stocks and bonds rather than fur coats." (*In re Marriage of Winter*, 7 Cal. App. 4th 1926 (1992).) Discussing the situation of the supported spouse, the Hawaii court opined that "the ability to continue to save and build up one's net worth is not a valid standard of living consideration justifying the award of increased alimony/spousal support." (*Kuroda v. Kuroda*, 87 Haw. 419 (1998).)

The bottom line: The courts in your state may or may not have taken a stand on this and many similar questions. There is plenty of room for disagreement. Find out your state's position, either through a lawyer or on your own. (See Chapter 5 for more on both of these approaches.) Depending on what you find, it may be a good idea to retain an experienced family law specialist to represent you.

My 40% Rule

When I was on the bench I had a personal and informal rule that, no matter how great the need, I would usually not leave people who were paying support with less than 40% of their income after they had made their child support and alimony payments. Without at least that amount, it seems to me that a wage earner has little incentive to go to work every day.

However, if the supporting spouse was the parent of more than four children and the other spouse had no job skills, I might well break my "rule" and go lower than 40%. I have never discussed this "rule" with other judges, but I would expect that many—although not all—would agree with the reasoning.

If you are presented with an order that would leave you with less than 40% of your income, point that fact out to the judge. But doing it as a veiled threat—"If that is all you are going to leave me, I might as well quit my job and move to Brazil" —would be a mistake. Most judges don't take kindly to those sorts of threats. Instead, try being a little subtle about it, such as: "The amount my spouse is asking for leaves me with less than half of my paycheck each month." And it may very well convince a judge not to wipe out "the goose laying the golden egg."

The Underemployed Spouse

As noted, alimony is generally based largely on what each of the divorcing spouses "reasonably earn." That means that if a person is deliberately working at a job that pays less than what he or she could earn, the courts will sometimes figure the alimony amount based on a higher figure.

For example, if a school teacher who earns $50,000 a year decides teaching is just too stressful and goes to work instead as a clerk in the post office for $35,000 a year, a judge might well decide to figure the alimony amount he should pay based on a teacher's level of income. And if a doctor making $200,000 a year in a big city closes her office and moves to a small town where she makes only $90,000 a year, a judge could base the amount she should pay in alimony on the higher income.

When facts such as these occur, the person who has changed jobs will usually be expected to present evidence on why personal factors such as stress made the change necessary. Sometimes a psychologist is called as a witness to back up the need for the change. The person opposing a reduction in support will often succeed if he or she can show that the lifestyles of those who are being supported will be severely affected by the loss of substantial alimony payments.

Court decisions in this area will often depend on the precise wording of the state law on alimony and the court's appraisal of the good faith of the supporting spouse.

A look at two cases on this issue helps illustrate. In one, an alimony-paying husband in his mid-50s quit his sales job to enter a monastery in anticipation of becoming a Catholic priest, at which time he would have to take a "vow of poverty." He testified he could not continue his former vocation because of stress-induced depression and that his conscience dictated he "follow a path of good works and services." His wife was employed as a nurse and, if she were to lose her spousal support, her standard of living would decrease somewhat, but not drastically. The court ruled that former husband could discontinue paying alimony, but retained the opportunity to reinstate it if circumstances changed. (*Marriage of Meegan,* 11 Cal. App. 4th 156 (1992).)

The same court, with a different group of judges sitting on it, criticized and declined to follow that decision one year later in a case involving a man who quit his job as a pharmacist to fulfill what he said was "a lifelong dream of attending medical school." The court denied his request to terminate alimony and reduce his support for two minor children and said that the good faith of the payor of support in changing jobs is irrelevant if he retains the ability to work at his old job. (*Marriage of Ilas,* 12 Cal. App. 4th 1630 (1993).)

It is difficult to reconcile the two cases because both cited the same law as supporting their decisions. Perhaps the major point you can learn from this confusion is one mentioned in the first chapter of this book: The result of litigation is often not predictable.

Waiving Alimony

Some states provide that the court will retain the power to order alimony indefinitely unless there is a written agreement to the contrary.

As a result, if one or both of you is agreeing to waive alimony—that is, give up any right to it—and your marriage lasted longer than three years or so, it is a good idea to hire a lawyer for just the limited task of drafting some failsafe language that will make sure that the alimony waiver will stick.

If you are set on not using a lawyer for any part of your divorce, but you want to waive alimony rights, it would be wise to turn down any opportunity the court provides for you to handle your divorce by mail. Instead, both of you should appear in court and explain to the judge that you want to give up the right to receive alimony forever. The judge will normally ask some questions to make sure you understand what you are doing and then incorporate the waiver in the judgment.

And if you have been married for more than two or three years and believe there is a chance you may need alimony sometime in the near future, think carefully about giving it up as part of a divorce settlement. If you were married for at least ten years and are over 50, it would be very unusual for a court to terminate your right to ask for alimony in the future. You can ask that it be "reserved"—which means that the court can revisit the issue later, or set at $1 per month—so that you can ask for a later increase if need be. (See "Modifying Alimony," below, for a complete explanation.)

Waiving Alimony: A Decision You Can't Change

Whenever I review an agreed judgment of divorce where both of the parties waive the right to alimony, I remember a friend who came to see me for legal help many years ago.

She had been married to a minister for more than 15 years, had been employed as a nurse, and was the mother of two young children. She and her husband had recently agreed on all of the terms of a divorce—including a waiver of alimony. Within six months of the divorce, she was diagnosed with terminal brain cancer. Her doctor thought she had about a year to live and she wanted me to file a motion with the court to obtain alimony.

Telling her that once alimony is waived, it is gone forever was one of the toughest messages I've ever had to deliver. But that was the law.

Length of Time for Payments

Some states have laws limiting the duration of alimony.

Delaware, for example, provides that alimony can continue for no longer than half the term of the marriage, unless the marriage lasted more than 20 years. California law states as its goal that the supported spouse become totally self-supporting within "a reasonable time" and that except in the case of a marriage of ten years or more, one-half the length of the marriage is generally considered to be a reasonable period. However, the law provides that a judge still has discretion to provide alimony for a longer or shorter period.

Obviously, you will want to check out the specific requirements of your state's law on this important subject. (See "Doing Your Own Legal Research" in Chapter 5 for an explanation of how to find the law.)

If the person paying support retires—usually at 65, but sometimes earlier—courts will often examine both parties' financial situations carefully to determine whether support should be terminated. Occasionally, a court will find that an alimony-payor who announces a voluntary retirement is decreasing his or her earning capacity too early and that payments must continue.

The Most Controversial Factor: Fault

While its roots go back centuries, alimony in its current form has been around since at least 1857, developed in England where divorces were handled in courts connected to the church. At first, alimony was ordered only when it could be shown a husband had mistreated a relatively blameless wife. He had been at fault—and therefore, she was thought to be entitled to be compensated, particularly if he had committed adultery or had harmed her physically.

And fault was once a factor in setting alimony in most of the United States. But the trend in recent years has been to get away from attempting to determine who was most at fault for the breakdown of a marriage, and to look chiefly at the financial factors discussed above, instead.

Almost half the states no longer consider fault in setting alimony. But in the states in which a judge can consider fault as a factor, its definition can be fairly broad. "Fault" has been found to include practices such as the earning parent requiring the stay-at-home parent to live on a poverty budget, being absent from home for long periods without explanation, or just plain psychological cruelty such as one spouse giving the other "the silent treatment." And in a sign of the times, a South Dakota court recently denied alimony to a wife based upon what her husband described as "Cyber Sex" on the Internet—she admitted "highly erotic discussions on Internet chatrooms with two different men"—as well as having an extramarital affair. *(Zepeda v. Zepeda,* 632 N.W. 2d 48 (2001).)

Fault by either party may be considered in deciding whether to award alimony in: Alabama, Connecticut, District of Columbia, Florida, Georgia, Idaho, Louisiana, Maryland, Massachusetts, Mississippi, Missouri, New Hampshire, North Carolina, North Dakota, Pennsylvania, Rhode Island, South Carolina, South Dakota, Tennessee, Texas, Utah, Virginia, West Virginia, and Wyoming.

In Kentucky, only the fault of the party seeking support can be considered.

The laws in Kansas, Michigan, New Jersey, and New York provide that a judge may consider "any factor that is just or equitable"—and sometimes that could include fault. This does not mean that fault will be considered in every case in these states, just that a judge who finds it serious enough can consider it as a factor in setting alimony.

The fact that many states have alimony laws that prohibit considering fault, or fail to list it as a factor that can be considered, can cause some awkward problems.

For example, every once in a while, the party who is required to pay alimony is pretty damn near a perfect spouse and not in any way at fault for the breakup of the marriage. And his or her former spouse may turn out to be a philanderer or addicted to gambling, drugs, alcohol, anger, or what-have-you. Can the innocent person really be forced to support someone whose habits or inclinations were responsible for the breakup in the first place?

Finding Fault With No-Fault

In a case I handled, an executive for a large manufacturer married a man who had portrayed himself as wealthy. Within a short time, however, she learned he was actually living on his small salary as a janitor. She might have sought an annulment when the truth came out, but she decided she loved the man anyway and struggled through a little more than five years of a very troubled marriage. When she finally sought a divorce, her husband became so distraught that he was fired from his janitorial job and had no earnings other than unemployment insurance.

At trial, the husband brought in an employment specialist from the Veterans' Administration who had tried unsuccessfully for months to find him a job. The specialist said the husband's ego was so destroyed that he could not participate in an interview successfully. His lawyer asked for alimony of several thousand dollars a month for an indefinite period.

The wife's attorney saved the day by obtaining an order that the husband must submit to a vocational assessment by a neutral expert. The expert administered a battery of tests and interviews and testified that in his opinion the man was a fraud, well able to hold a job and earn a decent salary.

Under earlier law, when fault was a factor, I might have denied him alimony because he had so defrauded his wife over the years. But, since the expert testified that he had the ability to earn a good living, I had the evidence to deny him on the grounds he had no need for alimony. That was my decision: no alimony.

The lesson from this episode? If you are requesting alimony, be sure your plate is clean. If you are being requested to pay alimony in suspicious circumstances, hire an expert to do a vocational evaluation.

In no-fault states, if he or she is the higher earner, the answer is "yes." These states were part of the "no-fault revolution" that began in the late 60s as a means of taking the bitterness out of divorce trials with the expectation that, among other things, it would aid in creating a better atmosphere for children whose parents split up. The philosophy has shifted in no-fault states from "he or she failed" to "the marriage failed." This can be a difficult pill to swallow if you feel you have been greatly wronged.

State Law Differences

Every state has its own law listing factors that judges there must use in setting the amount of alimony.

In some states, all the law specifies is that the judge should consider anything that leads to a result that is "just and equitable." In others, the list of factors goes on for a page or more.

All but nine states—Arkansas, Idaho, Indiana, Kansas, Louisiana, Maine, Mississippi, West Virginia, and Wyoming—require their courts to consider the standard of living the parties attained before they separated. And as attention to preventing domestic violence has grown, several states have listed that as a factor to be considered in setting alimony. (See Chapter 10 for more on domestic violence.)

The only state that has a precise mathematical formula for setting the exact amount of alimony to be paid is Pennsylvania.

Until 1995, Texas didn't even have a law providing for alimony. Now in the Lone Star State, it is available only under limited circumstances unless the marriage lasted for at least ten years. In most other states, there is no requirement about how long the marriage must last before alimony may be awarded.

Anatomy of a Law: A Look at New York

In New York, alimony is called "maintenance." The statute that defines it is found in a volume called Domestic Relations Law in Article 13, Section 236 (B). It lists 13 factors the court can consider in setting alimony.

Among them are:

- the income, property, and tax status of each of the spouses
- the present and future earning capacity of each, including any need for training that might have been skipped during the marriage—and might improve earning capacity
- the length of the marriage
- the age and health of each spouse
- the contribution of each spouse to the career of the other spouse, including homemaking, child care, education, and career-building of the other spouse, and
- responsibility for child care and child support.

Many of these factors are included in the alimony laws of other states.

Modifying Alimony

If your original judgment of divorce makes no award and does not reserve the possibility of alimony for the future (such as noting "the right of either party to seek alimony in the future is reserved") any prospect of asking the court for it later is probably lost forever. If the original judgment makes a specific award, such as "$500 a month until the year 2020," or specifies that it reserves jurisdiction on the issue, alimony can usually be changed—that is, extended, terminated, lowered, or raised—if either party requests it before the time it is scheduled to end.

To convince a court to modify alimony, you normally have to establish that some significant change has occurred in one of the party's situations—for example, the paying spouse lost his or her job, or the receiving spouse received a large inheritance. The change normally must be something that was not anticipated at the time the judgment was entered, when the court could have built it into the judgment.

In addition to the factors mentioned above, courts sometimes also consider the fact that the party receiving alimony begins living and sharing expenses with another person—legally called cohabitation. Properly presented to the court, this issue will normally result in alimony being lowered or terminated.

> **EXAMPLE:** If a marriage lasted for six years and the wife is finishing up cosmetology school while her mother babysits for the two children, a judge might make the alimony portion of her award run for her remaining time in school plus a month to find a job and then have it terminate on a specified date. But because there are all sorts of things that might change before she actually becomes employed, the court judgment might also give both parties the option of coming back to court before the termination date to ask for a modification.

> **WARNING**
> **If your circumstances change, high tail to the courthouse.** Most states provide that any change in an alimony award may be made retroactive only to the date you file papers asking for the change. So, if you are paying alimony and you are fired or laid off from your job in February, don't wait until June to file a motion asking that your payments be suspended or reduced. If you wait, most courts will not have the power to make any change in the period between February and June.

Enforcing Alimony Awards

It is one thing to get a court to order your former spouse to pay alimony. It is sometimes a tougher thing to get him or her to actually make the payments. If your spouse pays late or misses alimony payments, know that there are specific legal procedures set up for enforcement. (See "Violations of Alimony Orders" in Chapter 10 for details.)

Know What to Expect in Child Support

Simply put, if your former spouse has been given custody of a child the two of you had together, it is very likely a court will order you to pay child support of several hundred dollars a month until that child becomes a young adult.

It's a serious obligation, seriously enforced. In fact, a nationwide system has been set up to force you to make these payments, regardless of whether you choose to have any relationship with the child and despite the fact that the other parent may refuse to even speak to you. The federal law requires your employer to take these payments out of each of your paychecks and forward them to the custodial parent or an agency that monitors child support payments. If you refuse to cooperate, there is a very good chance you will be sentenced to jail.

And if you are the single parent who has custody of a child, you are entitled to free legal assistance to force the other parent to pay a healthy portion of each paycheck to support that child. Even the fact that he or she has moved to another state will not be a major problem. Every state is required to help the parent who has custody collect the court-ordered amount.

Child support is simply an amount of money that divorce courts order one parent to pay the other regularly, usually monthly, until the child reaches majority. Majority is 18 in almost all states, but is 19 in a few, and 21 in the District of Columbia. Payments are usually made to the parent with whom the child lives most of the time by the other parent, who may or may not spend time with the child regularly.

The law requires employers that are notified with a court order to make the child support payments on behalf of employees by withholding it from their pay. The order is called an earnings assignment, and the need for it is based on the fact that a not insignificant number of those charged with paying seem to give a low priority to child support. Without the watchful eye of the law, some would place their car payments or vacations plans higher on the list of financial priorities than their child support obligation. So this law places the obligation to pay child support right up there with the obligation to pay income taxes.

> **TIP**
>
> **A solution without a stigma.** If you are under a court order to pay a former spouse support or alimony, do not worry about a wage assignment having a negative affect on your reputation at work. The orders have become so common that many company owners and executives are subject to one themselves. For the same reason, if you are a person receiving child support, you shouldn't give in to your ex-spouse's plea to drop the wage assignment for fear a job may be endangered because of "this insulting court order."

As with many other issues in your divorce, such as dividing property and paying alimony, you and your spouse can simply agree between yourselves on the amount of monthly child support payments. A court will usually accept and enforce that agreement unless the amount is well below what the legal guidelines for your state would require. (See the discussion below, "Determining Child Support.")

This chapter offers a number of suggestions for you if you expect to either pay or receive child support. ("Enforcing Court Orders" in Chapter 10 discusses the specifics of enforcing child support orders.)

The Changing Child Support System

Before learning the details about making or receiving payments, a brief look at history may help illustrate how the federal government has become the major player on today's child support scene.

Once upon a time—in 1868, to be exact—the Illinois Supreme Court summarized the courts' role in matters related to parent-child relations as unnecessary, noting: "Nature has implanted in all men a love for their offspring that is seldom so weak as to require the promptings of law, to compel them to discharge the duty of shielding and protecting them from injury, suffering and want, to the extent of their ability. Hence the courts are seldom called upon to enforce the duty of parents." (*Plaster v.*

Plaster, 47 Ill. 290, 291.)

Of course, there are now and always have been many divorced parents who are deeply involved in promoting the welfare of their children. Many parents who do not have custody of their children—also called noncustodial parents—always pay their child support on time and even stand ready to do something extra when an emergency or a special need arises.

But these days, it certainly cannot be said that courts "are seldom called upon" to enforce the duties of divorced parents. In some major metropolitan areas, for example, a single department of the court spends almost all its time enforcing support orders.

Historically, there have been problems with child support: nonpayment, low amounts, unpredictable awards issued by courts. And while legal reforms have paved the way for some improvements, especially in mandating more uniform award amounts, problems still exist.

Nonpayment. Even with stepped-up monitoring and enforcement, the most recent report issued by the U.S. Bureau of Census found that 7 million custodial parents received only 69% of the $37 billion owed to them for child support by noncustodial parents. This was an improvement of 10% over what was collected in 1999. Only about 45% of custodial parents received the full amount of child support that was ordered.

Yet the trend in collections continues to increase every year as the collectors become more sophisticated in tracking those who attempt to shirk their child support duties. Very few regularly employed parents slip through the net.

Low support amounts. In the last couple of decades, experts have been concerned that the amounts of support ordered by the courts have been much too low.

As Lenore J. Weitzman wrote in her 1987 book, *The Divorce Revolution*: "Quite clearly, child support awards are not adequate to meet the cost of raising children. They fall short of every standard we have used: they are less than the average cost of day care alone, which would leave no child support money for food, or clothing, or housing."

Unfortunately, there has been only moderate positive change in the adequacy of awards—even in the face of inflating costs of food, clothing, housing, education, and other necessities. The guideline amounts for support payments in the lower and middle income slots don't even come close to covering the cost of raising children today. That's not to say that noncustodial parents in these groups are walking around with a lot of extra cash in their pockets. However, the disconnect shows that our society should make some better decisions about adequately supporting its youngest members.

What If Dick and Jane Need New Shoes?

Every year, the U.S. Department of Agriculture compiles statistics on the cost of raising children. The costs are broken into seven categories: housing, food, transportation, clothing, health care, child care and education, and miscellaneous—which includes entertainment and toys.

As expected, there are certain stages in a child's life where one type of expenditure may be particularly high, reflecting child care and education costs.

The following table, reflecting figures from the United States overall, breaks down the numbers up until children reach age 17—notably, before the time that the possibility of an expensive college education may kick in.

Annual Expenditures on a Child, Single Parent Families, 2005		
Age of Child	**Average Pretax Income**	**Average Pretax Income**
	$18,100	$65,500
0-2	6,080	14,000
3-5	6,880	15,100
6-8	7,720	15,990
9-11	7,140	15,320
12-14	7,650	16,230
15-17	8,440	16,670

Source: U.S. Department of Agriculture, Expenditures on Children by Families, 2005

Unpredictable amounts ordered. Nonpayment and low awards have not been the only historical problems with child support. When I was practicing law in the 60s and early 70s and it became time for a judge to announce his—there were very few female judges then—decision on the amount of child support, everyone held their breaths because there was no way to predict what the award might be. There were no formulas, no calculations. The amount of support was left to the discretion of the individual judge. Lawyers used to joke that one judge simply reached up over his head and pulled down a number out of the sky that "seemed about right" to him. But an award made on the same facts by a judge down the hall or another one on the next floor might easily be hundreds of dollars higher or lower.

By the time Congress took a hard look at the situation and passed the first major corrective legislation in 1984, the situation was a shambles.

Enter federal reform, which has carved large inroads in making awards more predictable by taking the discretion out of the hands of judges. For example, one set of laws passed by Congress requires every state to create mandatory guidelines for setting the amount of support that would apply statewide. It has resulted in similar cases getting similar child support awards in every courtroom in that state. The term "guidelines," however, is really a misnomer. It implies the amount set is a suggestion from Uncle Sam, when in reality it is a command.

As a result, there are many different formulas for calculating child support used across the nation. Some look at only a few factors such as how many children there are and what the noncustodial parent— usually the father—earns in an average month. Others include a host of additional factors, such as the custodial parent's earnings, the percentage of time each parent spends with the children, and the income tax effects of the order.

Many have listed exceptions to the law such as specific hardships that limit what the paying party can afford and what is to happen when the formula is applied in the case of a sports star or entertainer and produces a figure that is so high that it is clearly is beyond any amount a child would ever need. (See "Determining Child Support," below, for guidance in finding the specifics of your state law.)

The federal law does not establish any minimum amount of support, but just exposing the subject to statewide scrutiny has resulted in increases. A judge who was in the practice of customarily setting low child support awards now must comply with a figure set for the whole state after input from various interest groups at hearings.

A number of other new federal laws created agencies and federal funding for child support enforcement activities at the state levels. These reforms were long overdue and extremely beneficial to children all over the nation. (See "Remedies for Violations" in Chapter 10 for more on these agencies and some of their programs.)

Determining Child Support

As mentioned, the amount the court will set for child support in your case will depend in large part on the controlling formula adopted by your state legislature, supreme court, or other state agency.

Find Your State Formula

Finding the relevant law is not as easy as it should be. Hunting down the law that controls your child support obligation can be managed. Applying it to the facts of your personal situation can be somewhat difficult.

> **TIP**
>
> **You can hire someone to do this for you.** Before you read about how to go through the process of finding the relevant law on your own, be aware that there are lots of people—lawyers and other experts—who know the procedure in your state well. If you are considering using one of the legal self-help agencies or hiring a lawyer for unbundled or full service (all described in detail in Chapter 5), this could be a good place to begin. If you have all of the applicable financial information at hand, you should be able to buy an informed estimate from any one of a number of agencies on what the court will do on child support in your case for $100 or less.

If you choose to find and apply the law on your own, there are two quick possibilities.

You can go to the website operated by the National Center for State Courts at www.ncsconline.org. On the left side of the page, click on "Court Web Sites," then scroll down to the name of your state. When you arrive at your state's list of agencies, you will see a list of sites that are a little different for each state.

To find the information you need, look for a heading that includes the word "Home" or "Judicial Branch." Once there, you may spot a heading that includes the words "child support." If not, look for a Search box on the page, and type in the words "child support guideline." The court administrators realize that this is an important topic for many people—and more than half of them give good guidance on how child support is set, sometimes with a calculator that will give you an exact number.

As an alternative approach, you can go to www.supportguidelines. com, a website operated by Laura W. Morgan. This Virginia attorney runs the site as an aid for attorneys researching child support laws and guidelines, but it provides a good service for lay readers, too. At www. supportguidelines.com/links.html, "Child Support Guidelines on the Web," you can get a wording of your state's law. And "Child Support Calculators on the Web," at www.supportguidelines.com/calcs.html, indicates which court websites include free calculators—and also presents businesses that will do the calculations elsewhere for a fee.

Get Accurate Numbers for the Formula

The next task is getting accurate information to insert into your state's support formula.

In some states, all you have to know is your monthly income and the percentage of time the child will be spending with you. In others, you will need figures for items such as "unearned income," "new spouse income"—and money taken from your paycheck for pensions, health insurance, and the like.

You may have financial records at home or available through your tax preparer that contain reliable information on your earnings and those of your spouse. If both of you earn all of your compensation from employers who issue W-2 forms, this is easy.

But if either of you operates a small or privately operated business, things can get more complicated. You and your lawyer may want to subpoena bank or other financial records to be sure you have accurate numbers. If you don't feel confident you are getting dependable figures, you may want to retain a certified public accountant who specializes in investigations of this type.

Applying the Numbers to the Formula

Once you have the required numbers, it is easy to apply them to the formula.

There are also special factors that may be considered in some states—including hardships, educational expenses, high or very low earners, new spouses and new children. In some cases, judges have discretion about whether or not these factors apply and how to value them, introducing some unpredictability back into the formula.

For example, I have handled several cases involving highly paid athletes where the formula amount for child support was clearly unreasonably high. The applicable law states that the formula can be rebutted when "the parent being ordered to pay child support has an extraordinarily high income and the amount determined under the formula would exceed the needs of the children." In each case, I set support at a little over half of the formula amount. Similar provisions apply when a child has "special medical or other needs."

What to Do When Circumstances Change

Finally, be aware of changes that may occur for both you and your former spouse that may warrant changing the amount of support you should pay or receive.

If you lose your job, get into mediation, settlement talks, or court quickly to have it reflected in your support payment.

If you or your spouse has a promotion or a bonus at work, the same applies.

If one of you has a child in a new relationship, that will have an effect in some states. If it is the party paying support who becomes the new parent, child support to the existing children will normally be lowered. ●

Settle Child Custody and Visitation Issues Sanely

For many people, one of the toughest moments in the process of getting divorced is telling the children the bad news that Mom and Dad are splitting up. And if you think it is hard for you, try to imagine what hearing the news is like for your children. Your marriage, as rocky as it may have been, is most likely their universe, the structure for all of their important memories. So the news of a split is like a bolt of lightning they will never forget.

Surprising as it may be, more than half of a sample of children in one recent study reported that they were shocked to hear about an impending divorce. While most realized their parents weren't getting along, they had no clue they would decide to end their marriage.

Child psychologists say that when they first find out their parents are divorcing, many kids get the disturbing idea that something they did actually caused the split. The most common feeling is self-blame, such as: "If only I'd done my homework and gotten better grades, this never would have happened."

And the experts have identified several other worries children often have when they get the news:

- they will have to move from their home and perhaps live in a shelter of some kind, possibly never seeing their friends again

- when one parent moves out, the other may not have enough money for their food and other necessities, or

- they will be asked by some judge to choose which parent they want to live with and—once they choose—they may only see the other parent rarely or not at all.

Many children in their 20s and 30s look back at the time of their parents' divorce as the very most terrible part of their childhoods. Some tell counselors that because of that trauma, they doubt that they will ever get married themselves.

After studying 1,400 families over a period of almost 30 years, E. Mavis Hetherington and John Kelly state in their book, *For Better or for Worse—Divorce Reconsidered*: "Processing all the radical and unprecedented changes—loss of a parent, loss of a home, of friends— stretches immature cognitive and emotional abilities to the absolute limit and sometimes beyond that limit." And yet, they add that, "children can be protected by vigorous, involved, competent parenting."

Keeping down the level of conflict between you and your spouse during and after divorce is the very best way to prevent your children from carrying injuries that can affect them for the rest of their lives.

And, even if your spouse is too insensitive to understand what a tragedy a divorce is for a child, you still have the duty to do everything you can to lessen the damage for your kids. One parent described his role in protecting his children as "something like a soldier throwing himself over a hand grenade to save someone important from being killed." That's a bit dramatic, but it captures the idea.

Of course, there are many situations in troubled marriages where filing for divorce is actually one of the kindest and most beneficial things that can be done for a child who is being abused, neglected, or ignored. And a parent's alcohol or drug abuse and uncontrolled anger should not be part of any child's life. Such troubled parents often make many promises to reform, but real change is unusual unless they get very involved with a professional counselor or an organization such as Alcoholics Anonymous.

RESOURCES
The most recent book by Judith Wallerstein, who has cowritten four books on children and divorce, is *What About the Kids?: Raising Your Children Before, During and After Divorce* (Hyperion). It discusses in detail the best way to tell children about an impending divorce—including excellent word-for-word approaches for specific age groups, from babies to college students.

The American Bar Association (ABA) publishes an excellent paperback issue excerpted from its magazine, *Family Advocate*, discussing many aspects of dealing with children during a divorce. It includes subjects such as "Does My Child Get to Speak With the Judge?" and "Who Represents Your Child?" The book, entitled *What Your Children Need . . . Now!*, is available from the ABA at 800-285-2221 or online at www.abanet.org.

The Case of No Second Chance

Sometimes the most abusive parents seem to be least understanding about the damage their conduct can do to their children.

I remember particularly a hearing in which there was evidence that a father had beaten the mother horribly in front of their child. At the conclusion of the hearing, I announced that all visitation between the father and the child was canceled indefinitely.

The father looked shocked and cried out, "What about second chances! Don't I get a second chance with my child?"

I shook my head, told him there were resources for people with his problem, and that he could bring the matter back to court sometime in the future—which was his legal right. But with some things involving children, there are no second chances.

When Good Parents Do Bad Things

The anger, frustration, and humiliation that often accompany divorce can cause what were formerly all-star parents to do some stupid things that add to their children's hurt.

Some are so bizarre that you may not believe that you could ever be involved in anything similar. But the father who broke out all the windows of the family car with a baseball bat while his ex-wife and three kids were sitting inside seemed to be a pretty normal guy who simply fell apart when the mother told him she wasn't going to allow him to take the kids on a long-planned Easter trip to visit his parents in another state.

Other instances of bad behavior inflicted less physical damage, but left their marks on the kids involved—and hurt the parent's cause, too.

- One mother, opposed to allowing her child to even visit with the father occasionally, disappeared with the child and was eventually found hiding out in a trailer in a small town. With help of a Wanted poster put out by the district attorney, she was found in a toy store buying Christmas presents for the child—and was arrested and jailed. I awarded the father custody.

- In another case, a father bought new clothes for his children during a weekend visit, but forced the kids to change on their mother's front porch before he left. He said the clothes he had bought were only for using when the kids were with him. As a consequence, I limited his visitation for a month, ordered him into a counseling program for divorced parents—and let him know he was on thin ice.

- And then there was case of the father who finally had some of his poems printed in a prestigious national journal. During a visit with his daughter, he read her a beautiful poem he had written about daydreaming about her sitting in school while he was working as a carpenter, pounding nails. The mom bought a copy of the magazine and found another racier poem he had written, but had not shown to the young child. The mother attempted unsuccessfully to convince Child Protective Services to bring charges against the dad. Then she brought a motion in divorce court asking that visitation with the father be halted. I denied her request and ordered that she pay the dad's attorney fees.

Many people, when they hear of incidents like these, have the same reaction: "That's terrible. I can't believe anyone would ever do anything like that to their children." And most people don't. But a look at them may act as a caution for you to rein in your own impulses at the stressful times that are bound to occur during your divorce.

By contrast, I know at least 20 divorced families that cooperate almost perfectly—changing visitation periods with a simple phone call and sometimes even throwing joint birthday parties. The children involved all talk with pride about how well everyone gets along. They are the envy of those of their friends who are part of an arrangement filled with hostility—and their parents are models, poster parents for how to deal sanely with tough issues involving children of divorce.

Parents Behaving Badly

In one of the most unusual cases I ever saw, the mom, who was a very high earner in the electronics industry, had moved out with the children—leaving the dad, a much lower earner with an hourly wage, in the family home. She sent the kids to spend a weekend with the dad, who was totally devastated by the fact his wife wanted a divorce. When the kids woke up on Saturday morning, they found this note hanging next to their beds:

"Good morning. I really hate to tell you guys this, but your mother will not listen to me and only sees things her way. I've tried to explain to her the way things really were here in our home but she only sees what she wants to. Maybe if you answer these questions she will have to listen. These questions won't have any effect on your relationship with either one of us. I've always asked you guys to tell the truth, now let's see if you're ready to become adults before your time. Only answer the questions you want to, and answer them honestly, please. It will mean a lot for what goes on around here in the near future. It will not have anything to do with the way I feel about you guys. I hope you already know that. Just circle one. Nobody will know who did each one. I'll do one, too.

Who do you trust more? Mom Dad

Who can you depend on more? Mom Dad

Who spends more time with you? Mom Dad

Who do you think lies more? Mom Dad

Who has been known to cheat on marriage or at least been suspected? Mom Dad

Who sacrifices more for the family? Mom Dad"

The questionnaire continued with more than 60 questions, including: "Do you think your Mom should give your Dad another chance?" The children dutifully answered the questions and the father faxed the results to the mother.

The Child Issues: Time and Money

There are two major issues concerning children that must be resolved in a divorce: the schedule for when they will be with each parent—called the custody or parenting plan—and the amount of monthly child support one parent will pay the other. (See Chapter 8 for a detailed discussion of child support.)

The custody plan normally includes a schedule of when the children will be with each parent, what happens on birthdays and holidays, and who provides transportation for the visits. Thanksgiving, Christmas, and other religious holidays and birthdays often end up being divided, sometimes with one parent having custody on even numbered years and the other on odd numbered years. And in some plans, for example, Christmas may be divided with one parent having Christmas Eve and the other having the majority of Christmas Day.

The custody plan also may include provisions for:

- regular telephone contact with one parent while children are with the other parent
- what school and church the children will attend
- what extracurricular activities they will participate in and who will pay for them
- which doctors, dentists, and orthodontists they will have
- who is not to be present during visits—for example, new romantic interests of the parents, an angry brother-in-law—and
- sleeping arrangements—including who, if anyone, is allowed to share the children's beds.

What's in a Name—and What's Not

There are some labels tacked on to custody arrangements that some lawyers and judges feel are important, so may also be important for you to learn. One is a division between what is labeled "legal custody," and another category called "physical custody."

A parent who is awarded legal custody theoretically has the right to make decisions for children about what school they should attend, who their medical and dental providers will be—stand by for the orthodontist—and other matters of that kind. Physical custody is supposed to govern where the child will live and day-to-day matters that don't amount to major decisions. As an added feature, legal and physical custody can be either given solely to one parent, or jointly to both.

Parents and their lawyers who are looking for something to battle over sometimes try to make the assignment of these labels an additional issue in their fights. But those who want to avoid unnecessary controversy often simply agree that both types of custody should be labeled as joint.

I have always felt that labels should not control who gets to make important decisions about schools, churches, a controversial surgery, visitation schedules, and other important matters. However, some judges feel differently—and give decision-making power on important matters to a parent who has been given sole legal or physical custody. For example, one state court recently ruled that a parent who has sole physical custody of a child has the right to move away from the area with the child. However, it added that the court has the power to restrain the move upon a showing it would be detrimental to the child.

The bottom line: Unless one parent has been irresponsible or uninvolved with the child, joint custody is preferable. If your spouse insists on sole legal or physical custody, it may be worth going to court to take your stand to oppose it. However, taking custody issues to court should be a last resort. Issues such as this are usually best resolved out of court, by mediation, or through collaborative law. (These approaches are described in detail in Chapter 2.)

Dealing With Disagreements

It is important to maintain as natural an atmosphere as possible for the children as they make the transition from being with one parent to being to the other. It is easiest for them to go back and forth from home to home when they have the sincere best wishes of each parent. If you can't be sincere, at least do the best you can to reassure the children that it is fine with you that they love and spend time with their other parent.

But when parents can't cloak their hostility to one another, as is too often the case, all sorts of accommodations for exchanging the children can be arranged. Sometimes a grandparent's house is used. Sometimes more complicated details are involved. For example, a plan may specify that the visiting parent is to park in front of the other parent's home, remain in the car, and honk twice. The other parent should then open the front door to let the child out, but remain in the doorway. No words other than "Goodbye" or "Have a good time" are to be spoken. One parent in such a plan said that he was sorry these regulations were necessary. "But I hate their mother so much," he explained, "that I cannot be in her presence without losing all control of my behavior."

In very hostile cases, lawyers sometimes ask to have the court order the exchange to be made in the lobby of the local police department.

In some difficult cases, the custody plans provide that neither parent can disparage the other in the presence of the children and that the children shall not be used to carry messages between the parents— although these are hard to enforce in reality. In cases in which a child has serious asthma or other medical condition, detailed medical procedures and administration of medicines are often included in the plans.

Services Borne From Hostility

Because of the hostility that develops between some parents, public and private agencies have sprung up to fill a need. In such arrangements, one parent commonly delivers the child to the headquarters of an agency or local hospital 15 minutes before the other parent is to pick him or her up for a visit.

Toys and books are provided to occupy the child between the time one parent leaves and the other arrives. And if the child is young and doesn't feel entirely comfortable with the visiting parent, an escort may accompany the child and parent to a nearby park or other spot for the visit. Records of the visits and exchanges are maintained for possible use in court.

Obviously, the fact that there is a need for agencies that provide supervisors for visitation such as this is a horrible commentary on the priorities of some parents.

And additional new businesses have grown up because of the poor communication that often occurs between uncooperative parents. Agreed changes in a visitation schedule because of sports, graduations, and the like frequently are not documented. Medical and dental appointments are sometimes missed because it is unclear who was to take care of the transportation. A solution may be to use an Internet service such as www.jointparents.com. It records agreements between the parents and provides picture swapping, expense tracking, and contact lists for them. It also sends reminders of what is scheduled and maintains a detailed history of what was agreed in case of a dispute.

A related organization is Kids Turn. It presents six-week programs for families going through divorce. The children are divided into groups by age and meet with counselors to discuss subjects they find difficult. Parents are divided into separate groups and have their own meetings. While the organization currently operates only in California, it also provides help in organizing programs in other states. You can get more information at www.kidsturn.org.

Who Decides: You or the Judge?

You and your spouse should be able to resolve the issues of custody and visitation privately or through mediation or collaborative programs. (See Chapter 2 for details on these.) But if you can't reach an agreement on your own or through one of these resources, the only alternative is to have a judge make the decisions for you.

The judge is given one test to apply: What is in the best interest of the child? The best interests of the parents are irrelevant.

Take the case of a mother who has primary custody of a child and plans to remarry a man who lives 1,000 miles away. She wants to take the child and move to be with her new husband. The child's father protests that his weekend visits with the child would be impossible. If the move is allowed, the child will have to change schools, lose friends, and see the father only irregularly. Situations like this have become more frequent in recent years as our society becomes more mobile and employers transfer their employees around the world.

I have decided many cases with similar themes, some for the parent who moved, some for the stay-at-home parent. In one case in which I denied a move similar to the situation described above, the mother canceled the wedding to avoid losing substantial time with her child.

Be aware that when you take child issues to court, you are turning over complete control of major elements of their future to a judge who doesn't know you or your children. In most cases, the judge has had little or no training in child development or psychology.

And also bear in mind that any agreement that brings goodwill for people who will always be part of your family is miles ahead of something a judge imposes. As your child grows and changes, it will be much simpler to modify an agreement that the parents are able to reach on their own.

For example, you may want to take your children on a special extended vacation some day. It will be much easier to arrange if there is a history of agreements of this type between you and your ex. But without an agreement, the matter must be settled by a judge. And that will involve legal maneuvering, including preparing documents that will get you on the court calendar, gathering evidence supporting your request, and appearing at a hearing in court. Lawyer fees for such a matter will normally exceed $2,500.

Wisdom From the Bench

Judge Thomas R. Murphy, now retired from a San Diego Superior Court, says he began every child custody trial that was assigned to his courtroom with the following speech, which summarizes the reality, pain, and possibility in every court-determined case involving custody and visitation issues.

"The two of you are asking me to decide some very important issues affecting the lives of your children. That's going to be a bit difficult because, although I'll hear from you about these children, I won't personally ever know you or them. Unlike you, I don't love your children and I never will. Unfortunately, you know subtle little things difficult to put into words about what is best for your children—things that will never come out here in court.

"Proceeding with a trial on these issues is going to cost you quite a bit in attorney's fees—that's money that could otherwise be spent for your children's college education. Before going ahead with a trial, you should consider carefully whose college education you want to pay for—your children's or your attorney's children's.

"Before we get started, I want you to go with your attorneys into the conference room across the hall and make one last attempt to agree on a custody plan that is best for your children. If you are not able to do so, come back into court and I will make those decisions for you.

"My decision will not be nearly as good as any plan the two of you agree upon. But I will do it if you can't."

Mediating the Issues

One of the prime benefits of using methods other than court to resolve parenting issues is that they promote more realistic custody plans. (See Chapter 2 for details.) There are some mediators who specialize in doing this as part of the divorce procedure.

Experts disagree over whether children should participate in the custody phases of divorce mediation. Of course, the maturity and temperament of a child will control the answer in many cases. Discuss this subject with your mediator, who may have some standard practice for dealing with it. Obviously, children should not be burdened with decisions that should be decided by their parents. But discussing various custody and visitation schedules with children who are sufficiently mature may help avoid problems that could sabotage a plan for reasons parents might not anticipate.

Even if the children don't participate in the actual mediation, some experts feel that it can be important to have a mature child present when the final mediated agreement is signed. It can provide a sense that, despite lingering hopes a child may have, the marriage is really over, but that Mom and Dad are still taking care of them.

RESOURCES

An excellent book answering questions you may have about mediation is *Divorce Without Court: A Guide to Mediation & Divorce*, by Katherine E. Stoner (Nolo). The book discusses important questions about approaching your spouse about the subject of mediation, finding the best private mediator for your case, and the availability of court-sponsored mediation programs.

Using Evaluators

An expensive, but often effective way to avoid a custody battle in court is for you or your lawyers to agree on a neutral expert to do a custody evaluation and make a recommendation to the court. The cost often exceeds $5,000.

Most large communities have a corps of private mental health professionals—psychiatrists, psychologists, clinical social workers, and counselors—who will do a study and interview family members, school representatives, and the child before recommending a particular custody plan. Home visits during which the expert observes the child at the home of both parents are normally included.

The advantage of using this resource is that an evaluator is able to look at the situation with a fresh eye and with the knowledge imparted by studying family dynamics and child psychology. Several people who have been through the process have told me afterward that, in addition to learning about their child's needs, they received a very helpful analysis of their own personality.

Sometimes a judge will appoint an evaluator on his or her own. And most divorce lawyers know this territory well, and often will agree on a person to do an evaluation. However, a parent is not required to accept a recommended plan, and sometimes will oppose it. This may require hiring a competing expert to challenge the recommendation of the first expert, a move that is rarely successful.

Custody Plan Basics

A custody plan sets the schedule for the child's year, including holidays and vacations. It may also set out a method for resolving disagreements and for modifying the original plan to adapt to changing needs over the years.

ADDITIONAL RESOURCES
Specifics of custody and other plans are discussed in *Child Custody: Building Parenting Agreements That Work*, by Mimi Lyster (Nolo).

Scheduling Times

Figuring out when your child is going to be with which parent is almost always the toughest issue to resolve in a custody plan.

Some of the custody schedules parents work out are so complex that it is easy to understand why children become confused about where home is when they get out of school at the end of a day. It's usually easier when the plan provides alternate weeks or months from one household to the other, sometimes even maintaining separate toys and wardrobes at each house. But when both parents work, weekends are a priority and complicated charts are sometimes required.

While the children are spending a week with one parent, it is common to schedule a midweek dinner with the other parent to break things up.

Pickup and return times also have to be specified, noting who has the responsibility of driving each way. If parents live a long distance apart, sometimes they arrange to meet at a park or restaurant halfway between their homes.

If there is more than one child, each one will have a different schedule.

For the sake of everyone involved, custody calendars should be clear and simple—and child-oriented, not parent-oriented. A parent who has a complicated life with conflicting appointments and out-of-town business trips must sometimes make a decision on priorities: Is it business or is it children?

Plans should, if possible, avoid long trips on crowded freeways during commute times. There should be fail-safe provisions for one parent to notify the other about being late or needing to cancel. I recall several pathetic cases in which a mother reported that a child waited for hours at the front window hoping to see a father's car that was hours late—and sometimes never arrived at all.

And then there is the complication of holidays and other special events. The most difficult seem to be Christmas, Thanksgiving, Hanukkah, and birthdays.

Separate plans are made for Thanksgiving, Mother's and Father's Days, summer vacation, and holidays for the birthdays of Dr. King and Presidents Washington and Lincoln, Halloween, and the Fourth of July.

Sometimes there are yearly trades, with one parent taking certain holidays on even-numbered years and the other on odd-numbered years.

Detailed schedules can be complicated, but are often necessary to avoid disputes.

The Family Home

Once parents have decided to get divorced, it is usually best that one of them finds a separate place to live.

The issue often turns into a dispute when the spouse who is the most involved parent asks the court for an order that the other parent move out by a certain date. Sometimes the other parent will object and argue that until the divorce proceedings are over, the two of them can live peaceably in separate bedrooms.

However, in ten years on the divorce bench, I never bought that argument. Try to picture what happens when there is a line waiting to use the bathroom in the morning. Or when the hamburger mom put in the refrigerator is used by dad for a quick meal. It seems to me the prospects for angry words and even physical violence is just too high. The atmosphere for children is gloomy and confused. Someone has to move out eventually—and in my book, it might as well be sooner than later.

> **TIP**
>
> **Some make the former family nest into a bird nest.** A few innovative parents have initiated a house sharing plan known as "bird nesting." Under this arrangement, the children stay in the house and the parents rotate in and out on a weekly or some other schedule. Sometimes the "out spouse" will move in with relatives or friends during the time the other spouse is in the family home. In other cases, he or she will rent a room or an apartment in the neighborhood and stay there in between sessions as the "in spouse." It can be a difficult arrangement, but it may make sense for a few parents totally committed to make things as easy for the children as possible.

Other Issues to Resolve

Related issues that divorcing parents must resolve involve quality of life concerns such as which school to attend and which of the children's interests and hobbies should be paid for and pursued.

Public schools in many large cities leave a lot to be desired and parents in such places often ask the court for permission to enroll a child in a private or religious school. They frequently want the other parent to pay half or all of the substantial tuition.

The parent with primary custody sometimes also requests contribution from the other parent for extracurricular sports, dance, music, and even horseback lessons. Again, it is a question of the ability to pay. This can be a particularly difficult issue where the child has shown a special talent for a particular activity. If money is tight, check into whether financial aid is available for such activities.

Enforce Orders and Deal With Violence Legally

Most of this book is devoted to helping you stay out of court. But orders to pay support or share custody of a child are worthless if your ex-spouse refuses to obey them. And an exit from an unhappy marriage isn't much good if you still live in fear of being shoved, hit, spied upon, or stalked.

Because of the anger, injury, and hostility sometimes generated by a divorce, you may need to ask the court to enforce a particular order and to set up rules for your former spouse's contact with you.

You may need help with legal orders in addition to those described earlier in the book, for example, if:

- your spouse consistently fails to pay court-ordered alimony or child support payments on time

- your real estate broker has sold your home on the terms that were ordered by the court, but the title company won't pay out your share because your spouse won't sign the deed transferring it to the buyer

- a court has ordered that you are to have visitation with your child beginning at 9 a.m. on a Saturday, but when you go by your spouse's home to pick up the child, no one is there and there is no explanatory note, or

- your spouse frequently comes by your home uninvited, phones you repeatedly at inappropriate hours, or parks across the street and watches who comes and goes from your house, perhaps becoming threatening or physically violent to you.

Courts have specific procedures to deal with these problems, but they will not take any action unless you, your lawyer, or some public or private agency follows the required legal procedures to bring the matter before a judge.

The Importance of Taking Action

Often, it's just taking the preliminary steps toward enforcing your rights that can prevent a bad situation from getting worse.

But I have seen hundreds of cases in which the abused party endures unnecessary misery for months without taking any action. A mom and children live in poverty because the support isn't paid. A dad's heart is broken because he can't visit his kids. A great offer to purchase your real estate on the terms ordered by the court collapses because your spouse won't sign the necessary papers. A wife sees her husband who has moved out of the house sitting for hours across the street keeping his eyes on the front door.

There are many reasons why people involved in a divorce allow these sorts of problems to continue. Some who are being harassed, stalked, or threatened are concerned that taking action will only cause a harassing spouse to turn up the heat and become even more hostile. And some fear that a local police agency won't have the interest or the sufficient personnel to get involved in a domestic problem. Some people may not feel equipped to confront these problems on their own, and hesitate to contact a lawyer for fear there will be stiff legal fees attached.

Again, although my strong advice is to keep your divorce out of court if you can, that advice does not apply to the situations like these. You should move quickly to bring these matters before the court. There are some fairly effective legal procedures that are available, and many communities have effective organizations to assist you free or at a low cost. Delaying action may expose you to serious financial loss, physical violence, or both.

Enforcing Court Orders

The tools that are available to enforce the court order you have obtained depend on what type of order you are enforcing. The procedures to activate these tools differ substantially from state to state.

However, there are two basic routes available:

• working privately with your own lawyer, or

• getting assistance from government agencies.

Using your own lawyer. Not all lawyers are familiar with procedures for enforcing divorce court orders, so if you decide to hire a lawyer for enforcement, you should inquire in some detail about his or her experience in this field. The advantage of following this route is that in most cases you will get much quicker action than in working with most government agencies. The disadvantage is that the lawyer will be charging you hourly for the time required to prepare the necessary pleadings and court appearances. There are nongovernmental agencies in many communities that will provide legal assistance for people with limited incomes. (See "Legal Help Other Than Lawyers" in Chapter 5.)

Using a government agency. Help from this source depends on what type of order you are attempting to enforce. Most agencies provide excellent assistance in collecting child support and frequently also do a very good job of prosecuting someone who violates orders prohibiting harassment and violence. Help is spotty in the spousal support area and pretty much unavailable in property division cases.

Below is some advice on what to do if particular types of court orders are being violated.

Violations of Alimony Orders

Orders to pay monthly alimony have the same force as any other court order and, if handled properly, can be enforced with the very real possibility of obtaining regular payments. If necessary, a court may jail a reluctant payor to show that it means business.

Some of the other remedies provided for parents not receiving child support do not apply to alimony. This is basically a political decision by state and national legislators, many of whom argue that that feeding the children is more important than taking care of the person who is taking care of the children. If you qualify for government assistance in collecting child support, some agencies will also tack on alimony collection.

A contempt proceeding, (described below), is always available in alimony cases, but in most cases will require the assistance of a private lawyer. If the delinquent payor has a good job or substantial assets, there are a few lawyers who will tackle your case based upon the very high likelihood the court will order that your attorney fees be paid by the other side.

The availability of an earnings assignment order, also described below, varies from state to state. If it is available in your state, it is an excellent tool that can often be used without hiring a lawyer for help.

Violations of Property Division Orders

If a court orders that your possessions must be divided in a particular way and your spouse refuses to transfer some item assigned to you, you can use the contempt remedy described below to force the transfer.

The court may order your spouse to remain in jail until he or she hands over the property involved. In some cases, if all that is needed to effect the transfer is your spouse's signature on a deed or other document, the court may order a court official to sign on behalf of your spouse. Such a signature with an accompanying court order should be accepted by escrow agents to close a sale, even without the personal signature of the recalcitrant spouse.

Violations of Child Support Orders

Nonpayment of child support is recognized by state and federal government as a serious national problem.

As described in the alimony section above, you can hire a lawyer to bring a motion in your local divorce court to have the nonpayor found in contempt of court and sentenced to jail. While in court, you can also obtain the earnings assignment order described below and set up progress reports for the court to check out payment performance after any jail sentence is served. This has the advantage of getting you quick and personal assistance and the disadvantage of being somewhat costly.

Because of the substantial attention that has been focused on the failure to pay child support, it makes sense for most people to at least explore the governmental help that is available. This means contacting your local child support enforcement agency and filing a request for assistance. You can locate your local office through the national Administration for Children and Families, which is part of the U.S. Department of Health and Human Services. On the Internet, go to www.acf.hhs.gov/programs/cse. Then click on "State Links," and then on your state. You will reach a description of the services available at several locations in your state. File a request for services to get things started.

The States of Nonpayment

The federal Office of Child Support Enforcement annually compiles statistics on the amount and collection of child support in the 50 states and territories from state-submitted reports. Below are the results for 2004.

State	# of Children Involved	Total Amount of Child Support Due	Collection Rate
Alabama	230,644	$2,499,632,027	50%
Alaska	49,682	$610,503,044	67%
Arizona	271,280	$2,043,831,587	39%
Arkansas	140,793	$754,154,762	59%
California	1,999,958	$19,311,918,483	44%
Colorado	150,616	$1,218,145,835	41%
Connecticut	200,788	$1,609,329,430	41%
Delaware	62,158	$254,060,301	49%
District of Columbia	98,054	$385,427,656	19%
Florida	810,814	$4,450,725,914	58%
Georgia	477,164	$3,153,110,463	42%
Guam	17,152	$98,686,387	58%
Hawaii	98,542	$592,384,830	31%
Idaho	105,478	$429,401,984	52%
Illinois	741,787	$2,793,325,607	32%
Indiana	353,847	$3,845,966,209	47%
Iowa	173,074	$1,071,650,175	78%
Kansas	142,008	$608,113,770	52%
Kentucky	322,568	$1,534,286,555	45%
Louisiana	303,306	$1,002,954,973	46%

State	# of Children Involved	Total Amount of Child Support Due	Collection Rate
Maine	69,059	$485,693,215	63%
Maryland	279,603	$1,567,171,221	54%
Massachusetts	273,598	$2,107,502,531	45%
Michigan	1,032,947	$8,972,572,657	42%
Minnesota	276,222	$1,566,019,740	64%
Mississippi	348,518	$812,377,470	37%
Missouri	382,074	$2,130,116,426	46%
Montana	41,884	$198,205,637	61%
Nebraska	111,393	$613,690,261	62%
Nevada	131,394	$923,619,653	54%
New Hampshire	44,194	$198,474,226	71%
New Jersey	357,924	$2,457,510,568	64%
New Mexico	82,531	$651,006,235	36%
New York	993,479	$3,999,544,112	51%
North Carolina	435,755	$1,735,238,083	64%
North Dakota	35,055	$166,101,123	59%
Ohio	1,011,119	$4,441,084,369	55%
Oklahoma	166,043	$919,090,608	49%
Oregon	272,160	$1,252,318,706	46%
Pennsylvania	751,910	$2,253,818,736	74%
Puerto Rico	276,598	$1,013,819,674	42%
Rhode Island	77,373	$190,954,666	30%
South Carolina	245,559	$1,185,268,288	45%
South Dakota	32,088	$139,664,806	55%
Tennessee	373,077	$1,943,718,443	46%
Texas	1,104,413	$8,977,955,095	63%
Utah	94,367	$342,017,300	78%
Vermont	27,547	$105,511,904	72%
Virgin Islands	11,580	$55,202,566	34%
Virginia	356,886	$2,194,136,831	59%
Washington	354,902	$1,972,615,096	73%
West Virginia	114,436	$841,158,565	57%
Wisconsin	346,504	$2,217,595,126	65%
Wyoming	27,790	$230,594,597	63%
TOTAL	**17,289,695**	**$107,128,978,526**	**51%**

Source: U.S. Department of Health and Social Services, Administration for Children and Families

RESOURCE

For more information on child support, see "Handbook on Child Support Enforcement," published by the Administration for Children and Families. Although it is geared to people who are working with the Child Support Enforcement offices to collect support, it also provides useful information to others. You can download a copy by clicking on "Publications" at www.acf.hhs.gov/programs/cse.

Violations of Child Visitation Orders

It there is a court order providing for you to visit your child or children and your spouse is violating it, your only legal remedy is to file a motion in court requesting that he or she be held in contempt of court, as described below. If the judge finds that the visitation order has been violated, your spouse may be sentenced to jail.

TIP

Possible help from our people in blue. Although it isn't an official route, some parents report that a call to a local police or sheriff's office will often produce helpful results when a spouse prevents you from taking advantage of your visitation rights. If you are going to attempt this, make sure you have a copy of the court order spelling out your right to visitation handy. Call from a location near the child's home. Don't say you are reporting a crime, but tell the dispatcher that you would like to have assistance in obtaining your court-ordered visitation. I have received some glowing reports of the diplomacy and assistance of officers who have responded to such calls.

If, on the other hand, you were entitled to a visit with the child and failed to show up, you are not in danger of being held in contempt because you are simply failing to use a privilege. However, it does provide your spouse with a good case for having your visitation privileges suspended or canceled.

Remedies for Violations

If you have difficulty in enforcing an existing order against your spouse or former spouse, the most efficient approach is usually to piggyback onto systems that already exist for paying wages and collecting taxes.

Earnings Assignment Orders

The most effective collection method, used to enforce payment orders against those who are regularly employed, is available in every state: the earnings assignment order. This is an order from the local divorce court directing the paying spouse's employer to withhold a stated amount from each paycheck and to send it directly to you or a monitoring agency you appoint.

It may also be used to collect from Social Security, retirement, trust funds, or lottery winnings from which your spouse receives payments. And it can be used to withhold money from unemployment insurance your spouse may be receiving. In addition, the order can include make-up payments to eliminate any arrearage that has accumulated.

If your spouse has a regular job with a legitimate employer, this method should be all you need to get the money. But if he or she changes jobs frequently or works out of a hiring hall, it probably isn't going to be much help.

Any divorce court can order an earnings assignment—and in many courts, it is done automatically when a child support order is made. In some states, it is also available for alimony. If the judge makes a ruling on support and doesn't say anything about an earnings assignment, you or your attorney should ask him or her to include one. Instructions on the correct form and how it is served on the employer will usually be available from the courtroom clerk or the clerk's office.

Intercepting Tax Refunds

Another procedure available for collecting on court orders to pay money is to intercept any federal or state tax refunds to which your spouse is entitled. Again, it only works with somebody who earns reportable wages and has taxes withheld.

This method of collection must be initiated by your state's agency for enforcing child support obligations. You can reach your local agency through the U.S. Department of Health and Human Services, at www. acf.dhhs.gov/programs/cse, as described above in the discussion of Violations of Child Support Orders. State sites are configured differently; if you don't find an obvious link to the information, type "tax intercept" into the Search function of your state site.

These state agencies have various other powers that may also be helpful to you. For example, many of them can act to suspend driver's, professional, and occupational licenses of those who do not pay. Passports can be withheld and sometimes missing parents can be located through the Federal Parent Locator Service.

There are interesting features in some of these state sites, including Mississippi's list of "10 Most Wanted For Failure to Pay Child Support," with mug shots. The site for Massachusetts features an alphabetized list of almost 24,000 parents (under the heading "Delinquent Parents") who owe more than $10,000 in back child support and have not made a payment within the past six months; it includes directions on the amount a delinquent parent could pay in back support to have a name removed from the list.

If the local agency you find on the website above is unavailable for some reason—such as being overloaded with work—you or your attorney can take the matter back to the court that granted you the support order in the first place. To do this, you file a motion for contempt, which is discussed in more detail below.

Again, reacting quickly to the failure to pay is very important, and, regardless of what your ex-spouse's excuses may be, you should institute some enforcement activity as soon as possible. It may be difficult to ever collect arrearages that build up if you accept excuses for nonpayment for more than a month or two.

Fail to Pay, Go Directly to Jail

In my years as a family law judge, I got the reputation for dealing harshly with people who violated court orders to pay their spouses support or alimony. If a hearing demonstrated that a person was in arrears without any good excuse, I normally imposed at least a short jail sentence.

Part of the way through my contempt hearings the bailiffs I worked with could usually get an idea that a jail order was going to be likely—and, if they thought the defendant looked as though he or she might not go peacefully, they would often order some back-up assistance from the deputies pool. Surprisingly, some defendants, and one employer who failed to withhold, seemed shocked when they heard me ordering them to spend immediate time in the county jail. And sometimes it took a couple of deputies to get the handcuffs on them.

I never had a case in which a defendant who had gone to jail for failure to pay came back to court later with similar charges. But I did have one prominent businessman who had served a night in jail come back to court several months later on another issue in the case. While he was testifying, his lawyer asked him if he had been taking care of some details in connection with transferring some property to his ex-wife. He turned to me with a slight wry smile and said, "Judge, after that night in jail, I am so careful about following rules that I even slow to 15 miles an hour when I go through a school zone at midnight."

Motion for Contempt

The workhorse for enforcement in divorce court is the motion for contempt. It is sometimes called an Order to Show Cause re Contempt, which does the same thing, with a slightly different procedural status.

The motion simply recites how the respondent violated a court order and asks that the judge sentence him or her to jail.

To win a contempt order, you must prove that your former spouse:

• knew of the court order

• had the ability to comply with it, and

• violated the order.

Knowledge of the order. This is easiest to prove if there is a written court order specifying exactly when the visitation is to occur and it is clear your spouse received a copy of the order. It is usually sufficient to simply prove he or she was in court when the judge announced the order.

Ability to comply. In visitation cases, this is rarely an issue. For example, if your spouse was unable to be present because he or she was stranded across the country on a day when planes weren't flying, then a judge might well find there was no ability to comply. However, in support and alimony cases, ability to comply is often a hotly contested matter. If the spouse who was ordered to pay support is out of work and without resources, he or she can argue there is an inability to comply.

The spouse who wants the payments can rebut this by showing that the unemployed spouse had an "earning capacity" and failed to go out and seek work or ignored reasonable opportunities to obtain work. Rather than put a potential provider with job skills in jail, some judges will order that person to come back to court once a week at an assigned time with a list of at least ten places he or she applied for work with the name and phone number of the person who took each application.

Violation of the order. If you showed up for your visitation two hours late and your spouse had taken your disappointed child to the zoo, he or she probably will not be found to have violated the order by failing to have the child present as promised. In support cases, late payments may or may not be found to be a violation, depending on the circumstances. Failing to make even a partial payment—$100 on what was supposed to be $350—will usually call for a jail sentence.

While some people prepare and present contempt motions without the help of a lawyer, a lawyer who is experienced in marshaling and presenting the elements of the offense can make a matter such as this pretty simple. (See Chapter 5 for guidance on finding and hiring a lawyer.)

It is considerably more difficult for a person without a lawyer because the defendant almost certainly will have one. Because the person charged with contempt is facing a possible jail sentence, if he or she cannot afford a lawyer, the county will appoint one.

It is the job of the opposing lawyer to attempt to tie up an unrepresented person with evidentiary objections that the judge may have to sustain. (See the resources mentioned in "Legal Help Other Than Lawyers" in Chapter 5 to see if you qualify for a free or low-cost legal help.)

One little-known problem in bringing a contempt action is that some judges are hesitant to order a party to jail when no ordinary crime has been committed. Instead, they rattle their swords and give the person who failed to comply a second or third chance to shape up. When asked why they don't get tough in these situations, some judges get pained looks on their faces and say something about the possibility that a nonpaying spouse will surely lose a job if he or she is absent from work while doing time. And some will claim that jail is just inappropriate in a tangled domestic situation. But, as mentioned, I have found that just one night in jail can bring some amazing transformations in how divorcing parties conduct themselves.

An Equal Opportunity Offense—and Punishment

I have sent some mothers to jail for not having their children available for visitation. After I did so in one such case while sitting on assignment in San Francisco after retirement, miffed supporters held a held a protest against me complete with signs suggesting I was "Anti Mothers" and "Pro Fathers."

If they'd checked a little, they would have discovered a father's group had earlier attempted to have me removed from office, claiming I was prejudiced against fathers, as evidenced by the harsh sentences I imposed on them.

Dealing With Domestic Violence

The definition of domestic violence varies somewhat from state to state, but generally it includes any action that one person takes to harass, attack, strike, threaten, assault—sexually or physically assault, hit, follow, stalk, molest, destroy personal possessions, disturb the peace, keep under surveillance, or block movements of another person.

To qualify as domestic rather than other types of violence, the person committing it must be someone to whom you now are or previously were married. In some states, it also includes people to whom you are related, lived with, had a child with, or perhaps simply dated.

Courts may intervene in these situations by issuing orders that specifically ban any of the actions described above. These "restraining orders" may prohibit the perpetrator from contacting you personally or by telephone, mail, or email. The person may even be restrained from attempting to find you or your family members. He or she may also be restrained from coming within a stated distance—such as 100 yards—from you or others, your home, your vehicle, your job or workplace, and your child's school or child care location. And the person may be ordered to move out of a house or apartment immediately or by a certain date. An order may also deal with financial matters and require the wrongdoer to participate in a domestic violence or anger management program.

The time when police brushed off domestic violence as "a family matter" beyond their jurisdiction has pretty well disappeared—and most departments in even relatively small communities require officers to be trained to recognize and make arrests for domestic violence. Of course, there still are a few officers who are less than helpful, and some areas in which budget problems mean that police response time to a domestic violence call is unacceptably long. But both training and response time have improved substantially in most places during the last decade or so.

Witness to a Domestic Call Response

One Sunday morning a few years ago, a woman who lived with her husband next door to me called and asked if I could come over to her house quickly. When I arrived, she explained that her husband had just made some violent threats to her and then had sped away in his car. She had called the police and asked me to stay until an officer arrived.

An officer was there within ten minutes. As he walked in, I started to introduce myself. But he looked at me sternly and told me to sit down and be quiet until he called on me. He then conducted a thorough interview of the woman, got a phone number for a place she thought her husband might be, and dialed the number. When he got an answering machine, he barked out a direction that the man stay 100 yards away from the house and have no further contact with his wife for several days. He said officers on the beat would be informed to arrest him if he was found in the area. He instructed the woman about how to get a formal restraining order the next day.

Then, he turned to me and gruffly asked what my role in all of this was. I said I was a neighbor, handed him my judicial identification card—and told him how much I admired the way he had handled the situation. Shaking his head and smiling, he said something about how a police officer never knew who he may be performing before. I followed up with a glowing letter to the police chief.

Criminal Versus Civil Actions

Domestic violence matters are handled in some areas in both in the criminal division and in divorce or special domestic violence courts on the civil side of the courts.

Criminal actions are usually initiated by a police officer making an arrest at the scene of a violent incident and the district attorney deciding to prosecute the matter as a crime. A jury trial may follow, and, if there is a guilty plea or a conviction, a jail sentence and probation will often be imposed. The perpetrator may also be required to participate in psychological counseling or a specialized anger management or domestic violence program aimed to reform his or her behavior. Because the defendant is entitled to a jury trial, these proceedings are not used nearly as often as the civil case described below.

Civil actions are usually initiated by a spouse or other person concerned about violence who petitions a court for a restraining order against the violent activity. This can be either in a pending divorce case or in a separate domestic violence action that he or she files.

The resulting court order may regulate or completely prohibit contact by one spouse with the other. In many jurisdictions, a Temporary Restraining Order may be issued for a short period of time based on the sworn written testimony of one party without notice to the other party. A full hearing is then scheduled, during which the defendant has the opportunity to contest the requested order. Those who violate such a civil order may be punished by jail time.

Getting Help

If you are in the middle or a violent or threatening situation, call the police immediately. Just having a police car pull up in front of your house can sometimes defuse things quickly.

> **TIP**
>
> **Report poor responses.** In the extremely unlikely situation that a police officer who responds to your call refuses to take a report, get his or her name and badge number and go to the local police station to report what has happened. In most cases, the officer will at least take a report and refer you to an appropriate court office to follow up on obtaining a restraining order.

In less dangerous circumstances, it is a good idea to start with an agency in your area that specializes in dealing with domestic violence. Most Yellow Pages have a section in the front for "Community Services" or something similar, with a subheading such as "Child Abuse and Family Violence." If there isn't a similar section available to you, you might try the main Yellow Pages under the headings "Crisis Intervention Service" or "Women's Organizations and Services."

An alternative is to call the National Domestic Violence Hotline at 800-799-7233. Workers there can give you advice about your options, including where to get help with restraining orders. They can refer you to local shelters that will, if necessary, provide a safe place where you and your children can live temporarily.

WARNING

Report violations promptly. Once you have a restraining order, it is very important that you report any violation of it to the police immediately. For example, if the order provides that your spouse is to stay 100 yards from your home and you see him or her circling your block or parked down the street, call the police at once. Tell them you have a restraining order and that your spouse is violating the order at the moment.

Get On With Your Life

S ome final advice for you in this final chapter of the book:

- Take care of yourself as you go through this difficult process.
- Get on with your life.

Taking Care of Yourself

Although I do not have training in counseling stressed-out people going through a divorce, I have been one of those people myself—several times. I have also seen hundreds of couples negotiate these stormy waters, both well and poorly, and have read several very good books on the subject. Gathered from these collective perspectives, this chapter offers a few pointers that seem to me most important.

Combat the Stress

The stress of divorce has been documented to have serious disruptive effects on individual mental and physical health.

Studies that were first published in 1978 have continued to rank divorce and marital separation second and third—just behind the death of a spouse—as the most stressful events in a person's life. Additional studies show that divorced people exhibit more symptoms leading to admission to psychiatric facilities than any other group. They also have more illness, higher mortality rates, and more accidents than married people. As if that wasn't more than enough, recent studies at Ohio State University suggest that the stress of divorce may also cause a breakdown in the immune system, which abates in the second year after divorce as stress customarily declines.

These findings do not doom you to suffer any of these consequences. But knowing about them can serve to alert you to the importance of dealing wisely with the stress you are likely to encounter. Accept the fact that the divorce process causes almost all people to feel grief over the relationship they have lost and that you are going to need time to heal. This is true whether you or your spouse initiated the process of divorce.

And in the meantime, don't expect to be able to operate at the same level you usually do. It is entirely normal to have trouble concentrating—being so distracted at times that you make mistakes. It's also normal to feel very emotional at strange times and in unexpected places. Try very hard to be patient with yourself, your children, and others close to you.

And keep in mind that settling divorce issues through the processes of mediation and collaborative law is a lot less stressful than going to court. (See Chapter 2, which discusses several alternatives to going to court.)

> **ADDITIONAL READING**
> For a scientifically sound and sensible discussion of the effects of divorce, see *For Better or for Worse: Divorce Reconsidered,* by E. Mavis Hetherington and John Kelly (W.W. Norton and Company).
>
> And for practical tips on coping, you might also want to read two fine books by Constance R. Ahrons, *Divorced Families: Meeting the Challenge of Divorce and Remarriage* (with Roy H. Rodgers, HarperCollins), and *The Good Divorce: Keeping Your Family Together When Your Marriage Comes Apart* (HarperCollins).

Maintain Some Perspective

Write out a list of some long-term goals for the next phase of your life, reminding yourself that your marriage was a major chapter, but that other important phases will follow.

And if fighting about a few dollars, who gets to keep that painting you bought on your honeymoon, or at what time you switch custody of your children on Christmas day is going to force you into a courtroom battle, think again about reaching a settlement that allows you to turn to that next chapter more quickly.

Taking Some Steps Forward

To help alleviate the stress you are feeling, try some of these time-tested fixes.

Get proper rest, nutrition, and physical exercise. Even if you haven't moved around much in years, try taking some brisk walks. This can be a great reliever of tension. (See "Find a Physical Release," below, for more specific tips.) If lack of sleep is getting in the way of your ability to function, see a doctor and get a prescription for one of the nonaddictive drugs that are now available. Force yourself to stay away from junk food. If you're not ready to cook for yourself, seek out healthy prepared meals in better markets and delicatessens.

Take a class. Local colleges and high schools have a menu of interesting courses that you have probably thought about taking for years—and becoming a student also offers a good way to meet new people.

Volunteer. There are likely to be many organizations in your community that are looking for people who are interested in their causes and who have a few hours a week to spend helping out. If you are interested in things medical, for example, many hospitals have excellent volunteer programs with varied hours available. If you have a soft spot for the homeless, check with a large church in your area for a referral.

A list of some available volunteer opportunities in your area is available online at www.volunteermatch.org, where all you have to do is enter your ZIP code, specify your areas of interest, and indicate how many miles from home you are willing to go.

Join a singles group. Parents Without Partners and other groups that welcome single people are listed in some Yellow Pages under "organizations" or "clubs." Many larger churches have singles groups—and even if they don't, they should be able to refer you to one. A local mental health association usually can make references to organizations that can assist recently separated or divorced people in reducing stress. YMCAs and YWCAs can also be helpful. And don't forget the Internet: Simply using a search engine and entering the words "singles groups" and the name of a medium-sized to large city near you will bring up many listings. Some of them are dating services, but buried within the entries are groups that you may find more interesting to you at the moment.

Stand Up for Yourself

Your goal should be to get through this divorce as quickly and wisely as possible. But keep in mind when settling the issues involved that you are not a helpless nobody who can be pushed into accepting results and alleged compromises that just don't feel right to you. Do not let self-pity, humiliation, guilt, or depression cause you to swallow anything you find to be unacceptable.

At the same time, remember that the breakdown of a marriage is usually not all one person's fault and, where it is appropriate, it may be helpful for you to share some of the responsibility for the demise of your marriage. Uncontrolled outrage about your spouse is going to make it difficult to reach any settlement. Compromising here or there on some issues is not a sign of weakness—particularly if it will allow you to complete the process and get on with your new life.

Find a wise friend to talk with about what is going on in your life. Or consider scheduling an appointment or two with a therapist to share your thoughts and help keep you grounded.

Find a Physical Release

You may have read many of the reports from the Surgeon General and the American Medical Association or possibly heard your own doctor touting the benefits of physical exercise on general health. And you probably have heard about how it helps people handle stressful situations, such as marital separation and divorce.

There's no magic to the type of exercise you choose: lifting weights at a gymnasium, walking energetically through a park, doing yoga, or digging a hole for a new plant in your garden. Participating in a team sport such as soccer or playing tennis or golf will serve just as well.

Get some regular exercise by joining a local health club or gym. Find a friend who will meet you for an energetic fast walk early every morning or after work.

Try to maintain a steady program at least five days a week without any cancellations for a minimum of a month and you may develop a habit that helps you through all of life's travails.

Getting Strength From Numbers

If alcohol, drug abuse, or anger control is a factor in your divorce, find a support group in which you can work on the problem with a number of other sympathetic and understanding individuals.

The success of Alcoholics Anonymous is legendary. Narcotics Anonymous and many other fine drug programs have produced similar results. You can find local groups in the business listings of your telephone book, or on the websites of Alcoholics Anonymous at www.alcoholics_anonymous.org or Narcotics Anonymous at www. na.org.

If you are hesitant about joining one of these groups, try just one meeting and decide for yourself whether it might be helpful. Before writing them all off as a bad fit for you, try meetings at a few different locations.

Although the research on anger management groups is somewhat spotty, many people have had great success with them over the years. For example, a very loving divorced father I dealt with several years ago had a serious problem disciplining his preteen daughter when she broke one of his house rules. On several occasions, he had pushed her across the room in anger.

I ordered him into an anger management group led by a local psychologist. The psychologist called me after the man had attended several meetings. "I really had my doubts about whether he could change," the doctor told me. But he then reported that something important had happened at a recent meeting. The father was somewhat proudly describing to the group how he had controlled himself during a new incident of rule-breaking by the child. He said that rather than using force on her, he had simply slapped his hand down very hard just in front of her at a table where she was sitting. It had frightened her, but he pointed out that he hadn't touched her. He thought the group of fathers would applaud him for his new-found restraint. Instead, to a man, the group members expressed shock and told him what he had done was cruel and excessive. He seemed rocked by their reactions. Subsequent reports I received indicated the man had remained in the group and was working productively to control his anger.

Groups of this nature are usually organized by psychologists and other mental health professionals. You should be able to find one if you ask any counseling component at your court, your county department of social services, or a family service agency.

Taking the High Ground

I was shocked some 15 years ago when I learned that divorce was about to happen to me. I felt all of the emotions that the books describe: grief, sorrow, depression, and stress. Within an hour, I was on the phone with my friend and running buddy, Don. I told him what was happening and we arranged to meet. In short order, we were jogging down a trail. Within a mile, I could feel the dark cloud over my head begin to lighten a little and the pain to become manageable.

During the ups and downs of the months that followed, hitting the running path with Don or alone was my best weapon against depression and stress. I know what physical exercise does for stress and I know it will do something similar for anyone involved in separation and divorce.

Walk the Moral High Ground

Although you may be tempted to seek revenge for things your spouse did in the past or during this divorce, the following words are among the most important advice you will hear: Resist the urge to get even. Concentrate on getting through the process as quickly and simply as possible.

You might even surprise your spouse by being generous on an issue or two—perhaps lightening your stance on monthly support or the kids' visitation schedules. Those who follow this path almost always benefit in the long run.

Seek Expert Advice on Technical Matters

Feeling confident about the technical side of your divorce can help you avoid many sleepless hours you might otherwise spend tossing and turning, wondering whether you did the right thing.

For example, if you aren't sure whether a proposed child custody issue is right for your kids, talk with a family therapist. If there are issues about the valuation of a business or how to divide an IRA, a stock option plan, or a pension, talk with a certified public accountant, an actuary, or a divorce lawyer. Even if things are fairly amicable between you and your spouse, consider having a lawyer look over any agreement you are asked to sign.

Manage Contacts With Your Spouse

You can often avoid a lot of problems by setting up some rules for when and where you and your spouse will have contact. The process of getting divorced can easily become more complicated if either of you is allowed to drop by to see or to call the other whenever the mood strikes.

Agree to periods of no contact and limit phone calls. If even such limited contact becomes too emotional, insist that communications be made only in writing. If your spouse is very angry or working hard to avoid being divorced, understand that this is not the time to attempt to reach a compromise on the issues surrounding the end of your marriage. Try to calm things down to allow reality to set in.

Keep the lines of communication open, but if you are determined to proceed with the divorce, let your spouse know as respectfully as you can that getting back together is not an option for you.

ADDITIONAL RESOURCES

A classic study on coping with divorce and moving on to being single is *Marital Separation*, by Robert S. Weiss (Basic Books). It is a thoroughly researched overview that contains lots of very helpful advice.

Between Love and Hate: A Guide to Civilized Divorce, by Lois Gold (Plenum), has some very good advice on managing yourself and your divorce constructively.

A classic, mentioned earlier, is *For Better or for Worse: Divorce Reconsidered*, by E. Mavis Hetherington and John Kelly (W.W. Norton). It presents the results of research involving 1,400 families over almost 30 years with many valuable tips on how to navigate through a divorce. It also contains authoritative information on how children of various ages are affected by the process.

If you have children and are part of the one-fourth to one-third of divorcing couples who may have difficulty avoiding a "high conflict divorce," read *In the Name of the Child*, by Vivienne Roseby and Janet Johnston (Free Press). These experts have made a valuable study about why some divorces become more difficult than they should be.

Getting a Taste of the Medicine

One of the many examples of a person taking the high ground occurred in a mediated divorce case I handled a while back. The parties were a dedicated mother and a very busy and personable father who owned his own business. They had two children, four and six years old, who loved both of their parents, but who usually saw their dad only on weekends and on the rare occasions he got home before their bedtimes.

When the mother filed for divorce, a friend told the father it was important that he seek 50/50 child custody and that he should make that a condition of settling the financial side of the case. He quickly altered his work hours and began to spend more weekday time with the children. The wife agreed to give him liberal visitation, but thought that there was no way he would arrange to be with the children half of the time.

In mediation, the husband was hostile toward his wife and unwilling to discuss anything else unless she would agree that he win the 50/50 formula. As the mediator, I explained to him that if we didn't settle the case, it was very unlikely that his trial judge would make the custody order that he sought. He remained unmoved and uncompromising. It looked as if mediation would fail and that the couple would have to go to trial. But as a last strategy, I offered to meet with each of them separately and to discuss their options.

In private, the husband was unyielding, repeating his mantra robotically. The wife, however, said she thought that it was more important for the children to maintain a good relationship with their father than for her to have a few extra hours of custody here and there. Besides, she said, he'd probably end up not using his allotment of the children's time. She was willing to agree to his demand to avoid a battle in court "just to keep the peace."

Back in joint session, the wife told about her desire to avoid acrimony in court, then agreed to the split custody request. The husband was so impressed with her concession that the rest of the case settled quickly—and no trial was required.

Avoiding Stress While Negotiating With Your Spouse

Court custody mediator Olga Paredes describes a process for preparing some divorcing couples for sessions in which they will be mediating, negotiating, or—heaven forbid—going to a court hearing. It may be little too "touchy feely" for some people, but I recommend it for those who dread such confrontations. Some mental health experts advocate using this approach in child custody matters, but it can work just as well in dealing with problematic property division or support issues.

If you are anticipating such a stressful meeting, find 30 minutes or so to be alone and undisturbed in a quiet place. Then envision the session in which you will be meeting—encountering your spouse in the waiting room, walking into a conference room together, hearing your spouse's voice, sitting through his or her version of what went wrong with the marriage, describing the needs of your children, and the like. The more detail you can bring to your imagination, the more effective this exercise will be. It helps if you can tune into how your body reacts to what you are imagining and then calm down through breathing deeply, relaxing your stomach muscles, your shoulders, and your jaw.

Experts say most people have no problem visualizing a tense, unpleasant situation. They ask people to imagine their best response to what is happening, to think about responding to the situation in a way that would later make them feel proud of themselves, and then to rehearse that behavior several times in their minds. The idea is to create a model of behavior and then to reinforce it through rehearsal so that it has a chance of interrupting bad patterns that make healthy communication difficult.

The goal is not to revamp your relationship, but to have some small successes in communicating so that you can work together in dissolving your marriage, and, if relevant, raising your children. A few successful meetings in which there are small changes in your own or your spouse's behavior can lead to hope of achieving the best possible divorce.

Getting On With Your Life

In several decades in and near divorce court, I have seen more than a fair share of sad people who can't seem to move on from their divorces. Some of them manage to turn the process of getting a judgment terminating their marriage from something that should have been finished in a few months into litigation that stretches on for way too many years. Others who have already divorced continue to find new legal issues or causes that allow them to come back to court and continue to fight their former spouses for many additional years.

And those battles are expensive. It costs the taxpayers somewhere around $30,000 a day to keep the courtroom operating. That doesn't include the cost of the building, the utilities, or anything like that—just the salaries of the judge, the courtroom staff, and the support group backing up the courtroom. If one of these divorced people files a motion over a question such as which school a child should attend in the coming year and then calls a series of witnesses to testify on that issue, the judge is somewhat limited as to how strictly he or she can limit testimony to move the matter along. Meanwhile, other cases back up in the hallway outside the courtroom.

Psychological Underpinnings

Some unhappy litigants who cause divorce proceedings to drag on seem to have chosen the ending of their marriages as the most important event in their lives. Some appear to be determined to use the courts to attempt to punish their former spouses. And some of them just seem to hope a judge will declare for all of the world to hear that they are good and that their spouses have treated them very badly.

Many experts say that some people have formed such a pattern of constant feuding during their marriages that they just can't break the habit. Those who aren't really sure they want to be divorced anyway may feel that losing their spouse is akin to losing part of their identity and that continuing the battle in court after the divorce allows them to hold on to what they consider an important part of themselves.

Clogging the Halls of Justice

The most time-consuming case I ever handled involved a husband who was an anesthesiologist earning an average of approximately $20,000 a month; the wife had a law degree and a Master's degree in business administration, but no significant earnings. The couple had one child and some fairly simple community property to be divided.

After a rather unusual spate of ten hearings on preliminary motions brought by the wife, it became apparent that it was not likely that the couple would voluntarily settle the remaining issues. During this time, the wife changed attorneys twice and began representing herself.

The trial on the issue of support alone, usually settled in two or three sessions, took 16 sessions in this case, many lasting for a full day. Much of the time was taken up by the wife attempting (unsuccessfully) to prove the husband was concealing income. She claimed that despite her best efforts, she could not find employment. I set support at $8,552 a month and, in hopes of encouraging her to become employed, provided that the amount would decrease every three months until it reached $6,672 the next year.

Over the course of the divorce, the wife or her mother—who joined the case over an interest she claimed in the couple's estate—had filed 20 appeals on various issues. Considering one of the wife's appeals, a judge wrote that his court was "on the verge of issuing an order to show cause as to why she should not be considered a vexatious litigant"—a little-used procedure in some states for regulating people who engage in tactics solely intended to harass. The husband had filed a declaration stating the litigation had thus far cost him over $400,000 in attorney fees.

In a recent check, I found that the divorce was still continuing, more than 12 years after it began.

Vivienne Roseby and Janet R. Johnston, clinicians and researchers in the field of high-conflict divorce, explain in their book *In the Name of the Child* that some people feel so betrayed when their spouses seek a divorce that their counterattack becomes the central obsession in their lives. They write that:

"With respect to loss, some people have difficulty acknowledging their feelings of sadness and mourning the end of the marriage. Instead, they seal over their grief with anger and try to prevent the inevitable separation by embroiling their spouse in unending disputes. Fighting and arguing are ways of maintaining contact (albeit of a negative kind), and even throughout all the fighting, these same individuals harbor reconciliation fantasies."

The Brighter Side

As tough as the process often feels, divorce also presents a golden opportunity to make some changes in your life and to identify characteristics you should look for in a future partner. The experts say that getting over a divorce takes many people two years, some even longer.

Carol B. Thompson, who before her retirement was one of the most respected child custody evaluators in the Bay Area—and, incidentally, my wife—says this about the subject: "'Getting over divorce' is a bogus notion. Marriage is a major life event and the impact of a failed marriage will have long-lasting scars for many very normal people. Instead of 'getting over,' the focus should be on 'getting on with life.' Not only is that a satisfying goal, it is realistic and attainable."

You can't really get started on all of this until your divorce is over, so my hope for you is that you will get through this process successfully having learned more about yourself and what you want for your future life.

Index

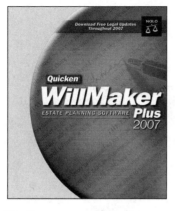

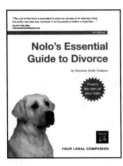

Nolo's Essential Guide to Divorce
by Attorney Emily Doskow

When faced with divorce, it's important to get the facts on every aspect. This book offers vital advice on protecting your interests and the interests of your child, and avoiding court battles. Comprehensive and accessible, it's indispensable to anyone going through this complex process.

$24.99/NODV

Divorce & Money
How to Make the Best Financial Decisions During Divorce
by Attorney Violet Woodhouse & Dale Fetherling

This book will guide you through the many important financial decisions that are made during a divorce, such as determining the real value of property, dividing debts, setting alimony and child support and negotiating a fair settlement. It includes easy-to-use charts, tables and worksheets.

$34.99/DIMO

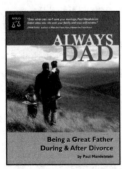

Always Dad
Being a Great Father During & After Divorce
by Paul Mandelstein

When going through a divorce, one of the most important things a father can do is maintain strong relationships with their children. *Always Dad* will help you do just that, with tips for creating a new home, developing new expectations, addressing kids' long-term needs — and more.

$16.99/DIFA

Get the Latest in the Law

1 **Nolo's Legal Updater**
We'll send you an email whenever a new edition of your book is published!
Sign up at **www.nolo.com/legalupdater**.

2 **Updates at Nolo.com**
Check **www.nolo.com/update** to find recent changes in the law that
affect the current edition of your book.

3 **Nolo Customer Service**
To make sure that this edition of the book is the most recent one, call us at
800-728-3555 and ask one of our friendly customer service representatives
(7:00 am to 6:00 pm PST, weekdays only). Or find out at **www.nolo.com**.

4 **Complete the Registration & Comment Card ...**
... and we'll do the work for you! Just indicate your preferences below:

- -

Registration & Comment Card

NAME _____ DATE _____

ADDRESS _____

CITY _____ STATE _____ ZIP _____

PHONE _____ EMAIL _____

COMMENTS _____

WAS THIS BOOK EASY TO USE? (VERY EASY) 5 4 3 2 1 (VERY DIFFICULT)

☐ Yes, you can quote me in future Nolo promotional materials. *Please include phone number above.*

☐ Yes, send me **Nolo's Legal Updater** via email when a new edition of this book is available.

Yes, I want to sign up for the following email newsletters:

  ☐ **NoloBriefs** (monthly)
  ☐ **Nolo's Special Offer** (monthly)
  ☐ **Nolo's BizBriefs** (monthly)
  ☐ **Every Landlord's Quarterly** (four times a year)

☐ Yes, you can give my contact info to carefully selected
partners whose products may be of interest to me.

JDIV 1.0

Nolo
950 Parker Street
Berkeley, CA 94710-9867
www.nolo.com

YOUR LEGAL COMPANION